SMITHSONIAN INSTITU
BUREAU OF AMERICAN ETHNOLOGY
BULLETIN 114

FOX MISCELLANY

By TRUMAN MICHELSON

UNITED STATES
GOVERNMENT PRINTING OFFICE
WASHINGTON : 1937

For sale by the Superintendent of Documents, Washington, D. C. - - - - - - - Price 25 cents

LETTER OF TRANSMITTAL

SMITHSONIAN INSTITUTION,
BUREAU OF AMERICAN ETHNOLOGY,
Washington, D. C., July 1, 1936.

SIR: I have the honor to transmit herewith a manuscript entitled "Fox Miscellany", by Truman Michelson, and to recommend that it be published as a bulletin of the Bureau of American Ethnology.

Very respectfully yours,

M. W. STIRLING,
Chief.

Dr. C. G. ABBOT,
Secretary of the Smithsonian Institution.

CONTENTS

	Page
Introduction	1
The Wolf Gens: How the Green Buffalo bestowed a blessing, and what happened to the one whom he blessed, from childhood upward	18
Notes	62
The one whom the moons blessed:	
Indian text	68
English translation	69
Linguistic notes on the Indian text	76
When the War Chiefs Worship the Wolf	79
Appendix	116
List of works cited	119
Index	121

ILLUSTRATIONS

TEXT FIGURES

	Page
1. Diagram showing the summer performance of "When the War Chiefs Worship the Wolf"	83
2. Diagram showing the winter performance of "When the War Chiefs Worship the Wolf"	84
3. Diagram showing the summer performance of "When the War Chiefs Worship the Wolf" (different informant)	89
4. Diagram showing the same performance (different informant)	92
5. Diagram showing the same performance (different informant)	96
6. Diagram showing the same performance (different informant)	99
7. Diagram showing the arrangement of the kettles (same informant)	101
8. Diagram showing where the wolf hide hangs (same informant as for fig. 4)	106
9. Diagram showing the summer performance of "When the War Chiefs Worship the Wolf" (same informant as for fig. 4)	112

FOX MISCELLANY

By Truman Michelson

INTRODUCTION

My excuse for uniting in a single bulletin the heterogeneous papers here presented is that originally it was planned to publish them not only in English translation but also in Indian text, for all were collected in the current Fox syllabic script. A variety of reasons have contributed to a modification of the original plan; and so only one is thus given.

The English translation of "The Wolf Gens", etc., p. 18 et seq., is essentially that written by Tom Brown, a Sauk of Oklahoma, many years ago. A comparison with the Fox syllabic text shows that the translation is close to the Indian original; consequently very few changes have been made.

A single informant wrote out the syllabic Indian text of "Notes" as well as an English paraphrase thereof. The English paraphrase is presented with some corrections in English grammar, and in a number of places it has been made to agree closer with the Indian text.

The Indian text of "The One Whom the Moons Blessed" was collected by me about 19 years ago. The English translation is based upon an English paraphrase written by Horace Poweshiek, corrected and supplemented by a grammatical analysis by myself. Some notes on the Indian text obtained from Harry Lincoln have been most useful in this connection. The Indian text is restored according to his phonetics. It should be mentioned, however, that a few manifest errors in dictation have been silently corrected.

The "Wolf Gens", etc., is precisely the same type of ritualistic-origin myth that has been presented by me previously. And what is more, the set speeches very obviously consist largely of the regular formulas of which I have spoken on more than one occasion. The performance of the ritual as given in the myth clearly is a reflex of what took place among the Foxes until recently, for it is some little time since the Green Buffalo Dance of the Wolf gens has been performed; and it has not been possible to obtain further details beyond

1

those contained in the myth. The tribal pattern for gens festivals, of course, has been followed. In view of all this, I have not given many annotations. The songs are given in the current syllabic scheme (substituting, however, roman type for the script) as well as English translation simply to identify the songs. It should be remembered that owing to the Fox method of writing songs certain discrepancies are bound to occur. The esoteric meanings of the songs are those given me by the author on another occasion.

Though I consider the author of "Notes" perfectly reliable, it may be pointed out that it is very easy to check the "Notes" in a number of ways. First of all, the names of the Fox gentes and various organizations are real, not fictitious. In this connection I may mention that I have rather full unpublished information on the Menstruating Society, including two lists of members, both of which tally closely with each other. Much the same applies to the White Wolves. I can confirm practically every statement made on mortuary and catamenial customs from other sources. Similarly I have often heard of children being told to exchange their teeth with those of garter snakes. The same thing occurs among the Mexican Kickapoo of Oklahoma. My former student, Dr. Margaret W. Fisher, has proved by documentary sources, genealogies, etc., that the theoretical exogamy mentioned on page 63 was the rule as late as 1907. There are also a few other statements which are confirmed by other informants and my own factual knowledge. The name Fish gens is given by the late Dr. Jones as Sturgeon gens, presumably more correctly.

The reproach (p. 69) of the woman that her husband had been lost because her parents were always demanding fresh meat is intelligible when it is recalled that in the olden days among the Foxes a young man often hunted 1, 2, or 3 years for his parents-in-law to secure his bride. (See Thomas Forsyth, An Account of the Manners and Customs of the Sauk and Fox Nations of Indian Tradition, *apud* E. H. Blair, Indian Tribes of the Upper Mississippi and Great Lakes Region, vol. II, p. 214.)

Several years ago I communicated an outline of "The One Whom the Moons Blessed" to Dr. Boas, who has incorporated a portion thereof in his Tsimshian Mythology. Dr. Boas pointed out that in an Ojibwa tale collected by the late Dr. William Jones the same plot occurs insofar as the number of winter moons is determined by the number of stripes on a chipmunk's back. (See Thirty-first Ann. Rept. Bur. Amer. Ethn., p. 728, footnote 1.) It is now possible to refer directly to the tale collected by Dr. Jones. (See Journ. Amer. Folk Lore, vol. 29, pp. 371–372.) For a Menominee version, see Bloomfield, Menomini Texts, page 335. Since the Fox, Menominee, and Ojibwa tales otherwise are totally different, it is clear enough that both have been adapted secondarily to the chipmunk episode.

Incidentally, although *Tamias striatus* is referred to, yet neither the Fox nor the Ojibwa seem to count the less distinct stripe down the middle of the back. For the Menominee see Bloomfield, loc. cit., p. 334.

Forsyth (loc. cit., p. 220), notes that the Sauk and Fox have 12 moons. His list is:

Tuc-wot-thu	Keeshis	First frosty moon commencing in	September
Amulo	"	Rutting moon commencing in	October
Puccume	"	Freezing moon commencing in	November
Kiche Muqua	"	Big Bear moon commencing in	December
Chuckee Muqua	"	Little Bear moon commencing in	January
Tuc-wun-nee	"	Cold moon commencing in	February
Pa-puc-qua	"	Sap moon commencing in	March
A-paw-in-eck-kee	"	Fish moon commencing in	April
Uc-kee-kay	"	Planting moon commencing in	May
Pa-la-nee	"	First summer or flowering moon	June
Na-pen-nee	"	Midsummer moon	July
Mish-a-way	"	Elk moon	August

Forsyth then continues: "Their year is quoted as the[y] are placed in the above list of moons, commencing with the moon that changes in September, being the time the[y] usually leave their villages (after saving their corn) to go westward to make their fall and winter's hunt."

Among the literary remains of the late Dr. William Jones I find a slip of paper on which the Fox months (in our order) are given, with some comments:

tcăgima'kokīcesōhi   Jan.: time when the old she bear makes the young stay out for a while so as to make it endure cold.

Păpō'kwīha   Feb.: time when it is warm in the morning and cold in the afternoon.

tăgwănīha   March: time when snow is frozen so that there is walking on it.

Pāpa'kwāha   Apr.: time when ice breaks.

Abāmine'kăwa   May: time when people return from the winter wandering.

A'ki'kăwikī'ce'swa   June: planting moon.

Negwătcikăwikīceswa   July: hoeing time.

Săgăna'kīwi   Aug.: time when the tops of corn come out.

Nĭbenwi   Sept.: ripening moon.

Tăgwāgikīceswa   Oct.: fall moon.

Tăgwătăhi   Nov.: time when everything is bitten by frost.

Ke'tcima'kwa   Dec.: when bears are mating.

Păgămăhi   Dec.: time when the muskrat home is hit with a spear to kill the muskrats inside.

[For some reason in the original Păgămăhi, etc., is placed before Tăgwătăhi, etc.]

On the back of the slip of paper is the beginning of a letter dated at Tama, Iowa, August 18, 1902. I here express my thanks to Dr. Jones for collecting these data; to Henry Jones, his father, for whose sake Dr. Jones was given the material; and to Mr. Wells, attorney at law, of Prague, Okla., in whose custody they were, for permission to publish them.

It is only justice to Dr. Jones to point out that this was among his early work, and that he had no opportunity of revising it before printing. Also Forsyth's list was not available to him, for although Forsyth's material is dated "1827", it was not published until 1912. My own informant could not read English, nor speak it, except very brokenly, and was entirely ignorant of Forsyth's list. Having these three authorities as a basis has placed me in a most unusually favorable position.

I wish at this point to register my high appreciation of Dr. Jones' scientific work. His paper entitled "The Algonkin Manitou" (J. A. F. L. 18, pp. 183–190) is outstanding as the description of the fundamentals of the religion of a primitive people. His translations of Fox and Ojibwa are in a class by themselves. His only rival, and possible superior, in the translation of Fox was his father, Henry Jones. I recall even now with astonishment an afternoon I spent with him in the summer of 1911. He reeled off sentence after sentence in Indian and then translated it into English with extraordinary accuracy and facility. And it should be remembered that without him William's own work among the Fox would have been impossible.

It will be noticed that there are strong agreements in the names of the months presented by Forsyth, Jones, and myself, as well as some disagreements; also the names do not universally designate the same months. Since Dr. Jones' list was collected 75 years after Forsyth's list and mine approximately 90, the above would be expected on general a priori grounds. However, it is possible to show that the disagreements are in part due to misunderstandings; so that the agreement is really quite remarkable.

Let us now examine Forsyth's list. The names for December, January, and February agree with mine (with the alternate name Tagwanī'a for February), bearing in mind inaccurate phonetics of Forsyth. These, then, may be considered as absolutely fixed, the more so because Jones' names for January and December (or rather one variant, Ke'tcima'kwa) also coincide. My names for December and January merely have "moon" and "little moon" attached. The same applies to Jones' name for January. Forsyth's designation for March very obviously corresponds to Jones' and my name for April. It is to be noted that my designation for March unless accurately recorded would not be far from the designation for April. The real designation for April may be considered fixed by the agreement of Jones and myself. The explanation of the disagreement of Jones and myself for the month March will be given below. Forsyth's term for April is either due to the editor's misreading of w for m or it is a misprint (read A-pam-in-eck-kee) and corresponds to Jones' and my

designation for May. Our agreement naturally settles the case; but
it should be noticed that since Forsyth gives the true term for April
as that of March, it is inevitable that the true name for May should
be given as that for April. For the same reason Forsyth's term for
May corresponds to Jones' and my word for June (minus the terminal
kī‛ce‛swᴀ). The term for June is either a misreading or a misprint:
read Pa-la-wee; this corresponds to my name for July for the same
reason given above. Na-pen-nee (July) corresponds to my term for
August (minus the terminal kī‛ce‛swᴀ), continuing the error begun in
giving the wrong designation for March (see above). Mish-a-way
(Elk) given as the term for August has no correspondent in either
Jones' list or mine. If this refers to the rutting of the elk there is an
error of biology: for in the Fox territory the elk rut in September and
the first part of October. Tuc-wot-thu, the term for September, corresponds to my term for October and Jones' designation of November.
Since Jones' alternate term for December corresponds to Forsyth's
term for November, and since Forsyth's designation of October corresponds to my term for September, I incline to the belief that the
names for October and September have been reversed. But it should
be mentioned that in Wisconsin (the earliest historic home of the
Foxes) the white-tailed deer rut the latter part of October and the
early part of November.

Turning now to Jones' list, it should be noted at once that the
names for January, April, May, June, and December (Ke‛tcima‛kwa)
agree with the terms given by me, ignoring the compounding with
the term for "moon" and some phonetic differences. It is easy to
see from the attached notes that Jones should have given Tăgwănīha
for February and Păpō‛kwīha for March. From the argumentation
given above it will be seen that I think Jones' designation for Sep
tember really is the name for August. Some other points have been
also brought out in the preceding paragraph. It remains to say that
there are a number of terms which are wanting in both Forsyth's
list and mine. These are presumably alternates; there is no reason
why these should not exist.

There is nothing in the lists of Jones or Forsyth that corresponds
to Wäpenāwikī‛ce‛‛swᴀ given by my informant as the name for
November. It is then presumably an alternate, or even an error.
I have indicated that I believe Forsyth's designation for this month
(with corrected phonetics) must be accepted. Also as the word
Tcāgä′nemetᴀ‛ as the name for February is not on the lists of
Forsyth and Jones, it cannot be the primary designation; the alternate Tᴀgwᴀnī′‛ᴀ is accepted as agreeing with Forsyth. It should
be observed that outside of Wäpenāwikī‛ce‛‛swᴀ and Tcāgä′nemetᴀ‛

there is no term given by my informant that is not in the lists of either Dr. Jones or Forsyth.[1]

In the summer of 1932 I obtained from an informant (now deceased) belonging to the War Chiefs gens a text in the syllabic script containing the names of the Fox months, and a brief myth accounting for them. The list is:

PApō‘kwī‘A, Ke‘tcimA‘kwikī‘ce‘swA   January.
TAgwAnī‘A, TcA′gimA‘kwikī‘ce‘swA   February.
Pāpa‘kwā′‘A ("ice breaks loose")   March.
Pe′ckunä′ ("blaze of fire starts")   April.
Ä‘ckipA′ge‘si′tA ("green one")   May.
Negu⁴tci‘igäwikī‘ce‘swA ("cultivating month")   June.
Nīpetä′‘A ("ripening month")   July.
TcāginAto′ ("everything is done")   August.
TA′gwAtä ("frosty month")   September.
PAgitāpAnwA (meaning?)   October.
Nāwatä (meaning?)   November.
PAgAmä′‘A ("strikes it")   December.

Harry Lincoln immediately corrected this, stating positively that Ke‘tcimA‘kwA was the designation for December, TcA′gimA‘kwik-ī‘ce‘swA for January, PApō‘kwī‘A for February, Me‘kwAmipāpA-‘kwā‘A ("ice breaks up [in the river]") for March, PA′‘kwAnīgi ("peels bark of trees") for April, A‘tcigäwikī‘ce‘swA ("garden month") for May. Otherwise he agreed with the informant. To a certain extent this criticism is just. For PApō‘kwī‘A as a designation for January cannot be supported by any other evidence; and everything goes to show that it is the name for March. Obviously Ke‘tci-mA‘kwikī‘ce‘swA and TcA′gimA‘kwikī‘ce‘swA are given with wrong values. Pāpa‘kwā′‘A as the designation for March is due to the fact that PApō‘kwī‘A is given a wrong value (cf. the error of Forsyth). But TAgwAnī‘A as a variant for February can be sustained; for PAgAmä′‘A=December (see above). TA′gwAtä can be sustained as the name of a month, and agrees with (barring the phonetic differences) the term given by Forsyth for September (which I think wrong; to harmonize the various schedules October will answer). It is possible that Negu⁴tci‘igäwikī‘ce‘swA (June) corresponds to Jones' term for July. The other terms stand by themselves; but they may be perfectly good, though unusual, variants. The term for February given by Lincoln agrees with that given by Jones (see the discussion above); Me‘kwAmipāpA‘kwā‘A is clearly basically

---

[1] As I write these lines I find among my unpublished Mexican Kickapoo data the names of a few months; unfortunately the informant could not remember all. Among them, the names for January and December tally with the Fox names; and an alternate given for February Tcāgänemä‘A [Ttka ke ne me A] is a nominal form corresponding to Tcāgä′nemetA‘, which is a participle of the indefinite passive. Since the Fox of Iowa and the Mexican Kickapoo of Oklahoma have not been in active contact for considerably more than half a century, in fact nearly three-quarters of a century, this alternate name must be old. I mention incidentally that there is a "rutting month" (A ma no wi ki de swa in the current syllabic script), but it is November, according to our informant. The names for March (O le tta gi a) and April (Ko ko we a) are alone thus far, as is the first designation of February (Le lo ni a, Winter).

the same as PāpA'kwā'A.   Other terms given by him are new to me,
but may be valid variants.   The schedules of the above are considered only here.

The following is a translation (by myself) of the etiological myth
given by the informant belonging to War Chiefs gens (vide supra),
which myth is of a totally different character from the one given
below (p. 68 et seq.), an additional proof of the secondary nature of
such myths:

Now verily why the months have names is that those who were
blessed, those who fasted, told it.   The brothers fasted very earnestly.
A long time ago they nearly died of weeping.   They did not eat for
10 days.   That verily is why they were blessed.   They were made to
know how many months there were, and their names in order; and
that the months were all brothers, and also that the months were
hard workers in everything they undertook; and that they first
planted all that we see.   And horses, cows, pigs, chickens, turkeys,
ducks, sheep, dogs were the pets they had.   And corn, pumpkins,
potatoes, beans, apples, plums, peaches, grapes, and blackberries were
theirs to take care of before the great manitous heard them.   Before
they started to take care of these, they blessed the brothers who had
fasted.   They showed the brothers where they (the brothers) were to
live, and what kind of places they were.   And they showed them how
to work their food.   And when the brothers had eaten they departed.
They went to work, and fetched what they had grown and fed their
pets.   For they had much stock.   They fed them all that they raised.
That is why they are remembered, because they were good workers.
And the months explained the people were given this as long as they
worked.   That is how the months blessed the brothers who fasted,
and upon whom they took pity.   And the brothers were exactly the
same number the months are.

European influence is clear.

For convenience I now sum up the names as I think they should
be given primarily, starting with January, though clearly the native
calendar started with either September or October:

TcAgimA'kwikī'ce'sō'A	January.	Penāwikī'ce'swA	July.
TAgwAnī'A	February.	Nīpenwikī'ce'swA	August.
Pāpō'kwī'A	March.	ĀmAnōwikī'ce'swA	September.
PāpA'kwā'A	April.	TAgwAtä'A	October.
Āpāmine'kä'A	May.	PAgAmä'ikī'ce'swA	November.
A'ki'käwikī'ce'swA	June.	Ke'tcimA'kwA	December.

The old names of the months do not function at all in Fox society
of today; English names, more or less Indianized, are in vogue; similarly the English terms of the days of the week have been adopted.
It is entirely possible that I have standardized the data too much.

I began to gather material systematically for "When the War
Chiefs Worship the Wolf" in 1917 and ceased in 1931 (summer).

Very obviously songs are still the great desiderata. As I have witnessed the worship in the summer several times, I can say that the general rhythm of the eating and dancing songs conforms to the Fox pattern. With a single exception (Kiyana, deceased) all the informants wish to remain anonymous. It is therefore proper to state that they are members of the War Chiefs, by good fortune four who belong to the ceremonial organization, and two members of the Bear gens who have witnessed and participated in the summer ceremony. The services of two especially prominent members of the War Chiefs gens, and of course members of the organization, were secured by the energy of Harry Lincoln, to whom I again extend my thanks. Two less important members of the gens and organization were secured by myself. It is well to state that their deceased fathers were both extraordinarily important members of the gens and organization. And a close blood relative of one happens to be one of the distinguished informants secured by Harry Lincoln. If we pool this information with the facts that can be gathered from the lists of the organization (see below), it can be readily proved that the key positions are practically all in possession of a single family, which tends to show that although in theory the ceremony belongs to the whole War Chiefs gens, in practice, it is not so. This, of course, falls in line with the strong tendency to interlocking "directorates" which exists in several Fox ceremonial organizations, as I have shown years ago. See also R. F. Fortune, Omaha Secret Societies, Columbia University Contributions to Anthropology, vol. XIV.

With a single exception (p. 88 et seq.; taken down in English; dictated by Harry Lincoln; informant a member of the Bear gens), all the information in the body of this paper was obtained in the current Fox syllabic script. Though I gladly acknowledge assistance from Harry Lincoln and Ida Poweshiek (Ida Snow Ball), the translations, barring the last document, are essentially my own (one is wholly so), and I think they are rather close renditions of their Indian originals. The case of the last document (p. 102 et seq.) is different. I regret to say that the Indian original contains a number of sentences which are broken Fox, as shown by a grammatical analysis. Under the circumstances it is not to be wondered at that Ida Poweshiek's English paraphrase was not as close a rendition as desirable, and that the broken Indian original gave rise to a number of misunderstandings. To remedy this state of affairs I have analyzed the Indian text where possible (and here Ida Poweshiek's paraphrase was of great assistance); so I have given as close a rendition as I can; but it is only proper to say there are a number of passages (which fortunately do not affect the general sense) which are none too clear to me, and a few passages which are wholly unintelligible to me. These last have been deled. So it must be said that the translation of that section is only approximate; but I think better than if taken down in English with no control at all. The same informant has written several texts for me in the syllabic script, and they all contain exactly the same type of blemishes; and can be used only as "controls." The "Appendix" is essentially an English paraphrase by Ida Poweshiek of an Indian original in the syllabic script by Kiyana.

The first five sections are by a very distinguished member of the War Chiefs gens, who has occupied for years a prominent position in the ceremonial organization of "When the War Chiefs Worship the Wolf." As long as the Indian originals are not given it should be stated that they are composed in fine Fox. The first ends rather abruptly. The name of the traditional hero KepäyōmāwA is well known to me (compare Bull. 105, Bur. Amer. Ethn., p. 3); that he was traditionally blessed with the ceremony under discussion is known to me from various other sources. A comparison with other Fox ritualistic origin myths shows that it conforms closely to the Fox pattern, and that the same formulas occur elsewhere. Sections 4 and 5 tell the same story. So do the others dealing with the ceremony which occurs in the summer. All this would be quite unsuspected by the laity familiar only with this paper. Professionals undoubtedly would be highly suspicious, even if ignorant of the published literature on the Fox Indians, unless indeed they belonged to that group of anthropologists who are only interested in how any given society, etc., functions today, and who are not concerned with how this came about, even if they by good fortune perceive that a historical problem must be involved. As I have touched on this before, I only give references to the following bulletins of the Bureau of American Ethnology, namely, no. 87, page 7; no. 95, pages 48, 49; no. 105, page 3; see also Proceedings, Twenty-third International Congress of Americanists (New York, 1928, published 1930), pages 545, 546 (where will also be found some data on "When the War Chiefs Worship the Wolf", which is taken from sources incorporated in this paper). It may be noted that data on the summer festival are more or less supplementary, rarely contradictory. The same may be said of the diagrams which are based on drawings by the informants (assisted in two cases by Harry Lincoln). It should be noted that nowadays the fire is outside the building proper at the east end, just back of the screen of rush, whereas it formerly was within the building, and some native artists have given the theoretic rather than the actual position.

Section 10 (p. 97 et seq.) is rather rambling in style, and at the beginning there is much that from one point of view might be omitted: it has not been omitted because it is quite in line with other texts from the same informant, and is conventional. As long as the "Flag" ceremony is mentioned (p. 100) I may state that the customary expression is "When the War Chiefs Raise the Flag." I have a good deal of information, most of which is as yet unpublished, on this ceremony, and this was obtained from several different informants, including one very prominent member of the War Chiefs gens. The same "interlocking" occurs of which I have spoken on several occasions. I have witnessed the ceremony only a few times. A member of the Wolf gens when serving as the head ceremonial attendant in the summer performance in a spirit of kindness gave me the name, Anō'tā'A, of the one who was traditionally blessed and who started the ceremony. The informants all ask that their names be kept secret. The summer festival is extraordinarily like "When the War Chiefs Worship the Wolf." (See also p. 546, Proceedings, Twenty-third International Congress of Americanists [New York, 1928, published 1930], and p. 15, Bull. 105, Bur. Amer. Ethn.)

Section 11 is not very logical. First we have a ritual-origin myth of the usual Fox type, then an account of the summer festival follows (p. 105 et seq.), the story of White Robe (WâpA'saiyA) who traditionally belonged to the War Chiefs gens (p. 108), then the account of the summer festival is resumed. This rambling style is quite typical of this particular informant (the same one referred to on p. 3 of Bull. 105, Bur. Amer. Ethn.), but since a good deal of Fox mythology and ethnology can be gleaned from it, I have decided to let it stand. The WâpA'saiyA tale is known in general from Jones' Fox Texts (see pp. 9 et seq., 17 et seq.). I have several unpublished versions of this tale (cf. Bull. 105, Bur. Amer. Ethn., p. 3). A very elaborate one by Alfred Kiyana gives a number of details confirming the present version. Na sa li lya ta, mentioned on page 108, is the name of a Fox warrior (belonging to the Fish gens, or Bass gens, according to the late Dr. Jones) who died a few years ago. I have otherwise no knowledge of a legendary hero of this name. The same applies to Ke ke gi mo a: It is the name of a Fox belonging to the Brown Bear division of the Bear gens, now deceased. Wi te ko ka A A (mentioned on p. 111) is known to me as a legendary Fox hero from a text written in the current syllabic script by Alfred Kiyana, an English paraphrase of which is presented as an appendix. (See p. 116 et seq.) The fact that Ke ke gi mo A (Kä'kä'kwimō'A) and Na sa li lya ta are otherwise unknown to me as legendary heroes does not in the slightest militate against their being such. For it is common among the Foxes (and presumably among the Sauks) to name males after traditional heroes. Thus MAmA'sā'A is the name of a Fox legendary hero (see Bull. 105, Bur. Amer. Ethn., p. 3); it is also the name of a Fox man who died a few years ago and who belonged to the Bear gens; so, too, Kepäyō-māwA (Ke le yo ma wa) is a Fox legendary hero and is also the name of a Fox man who died in the last "flu" epidemic and who belonged to the War Chiefs gens, and who formerly directed the dancers in When the War Chiefs Worship the Wolf (the hypocoristic

Kepäyō‘ʌ [Ke le yo ʌ] is rather more common than Kepäyōmāwʌ). So, too, Wâpʌ‘saiyʌ "White Robe" is a well-known Fox legendary character, but it was also the name of a Fox Indian who signed the treaty of September 14, 1815 (Wapasai, the White Skin; see p. 136 of United States Statutes at Large, Vol. VII, Treaties, Boston, 1848). So Wī‘sʌ‘kä‘ʌ, the name of the Culture Hero among the Sauk, Fox, Kickapoo, and Prairie Potawatomi (with the usual phonetic differences) occurs as the name of a Missouri Sauk who signed the treaty of September 13, 1815 (Weesaka, the Devil; see p. 135 of United States Statutes at Large, Vol. VII, Treaties, Boston, 1848); it also occurs among the personal names belonging to the Buffalo gens of the Sauks, according to the late Alanson Skinner (Bull. P. M. C. Mil., vol. 5, p. 23). When I say "legendary heroes" I do not deny that in ancient times there may have been actual persons with these names, but it is demonstrable that most of their exploits are legendary, not historical.

A word on "demigod" (p. 109). In the Fox syllabic text it is ma ne to wa ʌ pe ta we si ʌ which phonetically is manetōwʌ āpe‘tawe‘sī‘ʌ. Very literally this is "one who is half-manitou." For āpe‘tawe‘sī‘ʌ is a noun which is a participle in effect, and is based on the Fox numeral āpe‘tawi "half" (Cree āpi‘taw, Ojibwa ābi‘ta) combined with the animate copula -e‘si-, and then made into an animate noun.

In 1917 Alfred Kiyana wrote out in the current syllabic script the names of members and officers of "When the War Chiefs Worship the Wolf and Give a Dance" (translated very literally) which I now present, but substituting roman type for the script, the appended K meaning "Kī‘ckō", the T "Tō‘kān":

Me ne wa ki ma wa (K)   drummer.
Da wa te (K)   who knows the songs.
Ta ta la ko (T)   speaker.
Kya na wa (T)   who directs the cere-
monial attendants.
Ke le yo ʌ (K)   director of dancers.
A la ta o na (T)   singer.
Tta ki ta ko si (K)   singer.
Ki yo sa ta ka (T)   singer.
Mi da ka (K)   singer.
Le mi na (T)   singer.
Wi ta ka (K)   singer.
Mi da tti ne ni (T)   singer.
Wi ka me (T)   singer.
We ki ma ʌ (T)   singer.
Wa so se (T)   hummer.
Na na ʌ la me ga (K)   hummer.
Le mi ta no ga (K)   hummer.
Le ma na gi (T)   hummer.
A sa wa sa mo (T)   hummer.
Ne wa ki ki (K)   hummer.
Di di ga ne sa (K)   singer.
Ka we si ʌ (K)   singer.

He adds the following sit where children belonging to the War Chiefs sit:

E ni ka wa (K)   A no ta (T)   Ma ya tti (T)
Le mo se ʌ (K)   No ka wa ta (K)   A ge a ta (K)

If we turn to the list furnished by Kiyana it may be noted that all the men in the organization proper belong to the War Chiefs gens (see also below) with the exception of Tta ki ta ko si who belongs to the Thunder gens, Ki yo sa ta ka who belongs to the Thunder gens, Di di ga ne sa who belongs to the Bear gens, and Ka we si A who belongs to the Fish gens (or Sturgeon gens, according to the late Dr. Jones). It will also be observed that all the men save Tta ki ta ko si and Ki yo sa ta ka also belong to "When the War Chiefs Worship the Buffaloes" (otherwise known as "The White Buffalo Dance of the War Chiefs"; some recent informants have a marked preference for the first title; see pp. 42–43, Fortieth Ann. Rept. Bur. Amer. Ethn.). We have then the strong tendency to "interlocking directorates", to which I have called attention on more than one occasion. The hummers, who are females, always also partly correspond. Knowledge of the general principles of the Fox syllabary and that hypocoristic names occur is presupposed. The following will bring this out even more clearly:

Me ne wa ki ma wa, the drummer in "When the War Chiefs Worship the Wolf", is a member of the War Chiefs gens, and a singer of "When the War Chiefs Worship the Buffaloes."

Da wa te is a member of the War Chiefs gens, knows the songs of the organization under discussion, is a singer of "When the War Chiefs Worship the Buffaloes"; directs the ceremonial attendants in "The Dirty Little Ani" of the Thunder gens (otherwise known as "Those Who Worship the Little Spotted Buffalo [or Calf])"; he is the speaker in "The War Chiefs Raise the Flag"; also directs the ceremonial attendants in the Catamenial Society.

Ta ta la ko is a member of the War Chiefs gens, is a speaker of "When the War Chiefs Worship the Wolf", is a drummer in "When the War Chiefs Worship the Buffaloes", is a member of the organization known as "All Little Medicine Bundles", is a ceremonial attendant and head dancer in the Buffalo Dance of the Bear gens.

Kya na wa is a member of the War Chiefs gens, directs the attendants in "When the War Chiefs Worship the Wolf", blows the flute in "When the War Chiefs Worship the Buffaloes", is a singer in the Catamenial Society, is a speaker in the Red Stone Pipe ceremony of the Eagle gens, is a member of the Buffalo Society Medicine Bundles, is a ceremonial attendant of the organization centering around the Sāgimā'kwäwA sacred pack which belongs to the Bear gens.

Ke le yo A is a member of the War Chiefs gens, directs the dancers in "When the War Chiefs Worship the Wolf", is a speaker in "When the War Chiefs Worship the Buffaloes", is a singer in "When the Wolf Gens Worships the White Wolf", is a speaker in "The Dirty Little Ani" of the Thunder gens, is the chief speaker in the organization centering around A'penäwänä'A sacred pack of the Thunder gens, is a singer in the organization centering around the Great Sacred Pack of the Thunder gens.

A la ta o na according to one list written by Alfred Kiyana belongs to the War Chiefs, but according to another list written by the same informant is a member of the Fish gens, and I have no other statement as to his gens, but his membership in the dual division given is unimpeachable. (One son and two daughters belong to the Fish gens. The gens of another daughter is unknown.) He is a singer in "When the War Chiefs Worship the Wolf", and in "When the War Chiefs Worship the Buffaloes", is also a singer in the Red Stone Pipe ceremony of the Eagle gens, is a member of the Buffalo Society Medicine Bundles, and is a member of an organization which merely celebrates ceremonial festivals.[2]

Tta ki ta ko si is a member of the Thunder gens and is a singer in "When the War Chiefs Worship the Wolf", directs the ceremonial attendants of the Buffalo Head Dance of the Thunder gens, is a member of the organization centering around the Great Sacred Pack of the Thunder gens, is the drummer in "When the Wolf Gens Worships the White Wolf", is a prominent member of "The Religion Dance" (which corresponds to the "Dream Dance" ["Drum Dance"] of other Central Algonquians, and which was introduced among the Foxes by the Potawatomi of Wisconsin), is an important member of a Potawatomi buffalo dance which exists among the small band of Potawatomi who live with the Foxes in the vicinity of Tama, Iowa, which organization includes a number of Foxes, some of whom have Potawatomi blood.

Ki yo sa ta ka is a member of the Thunder gens, is a singer in "When the War Chiefs Worship the Wolf", is a singer in the Buffalo Head Dance of the Thunder gens, is a singer in the Thunder Dance of the Bear gens, is also one in the Bird Dance (i. e., Wâpʌnōwiweni) of the Bear gens, is a prominent member of the Religion Dance, and is a member of the Potawatomi buffalo dance mentioned above.

Mi da ka belongs to the War Chiefs gens, though his name is one that is proper to the Thunder gens and is "borrowed"; on two separate occasions he is given by Kiyana as being a Kī'ckō, but on a single list by him as a Tō'kān; as on this list a Tō'kān immediately precedes and follows, there is every reason to believe that an accident occurred, for another informant also says he is a Kī'ckō; hence the Fortieth Annual Report of the Bureau of American Ethnology, page 42, is to be corrected. He is a singer in "When the War Chiefs Worship the Wolf", also one in "When the War Chiefs Worship the Buffaloes", and is a member of the organization centering around the A'penäwänä'ʌ sacred pack of the Thunder gens (as is his father).

Le mi na belongs to the War Chiefs gens, is a singer in 'Wh'en the War Chiefs Worship the Wolf", also one in "When the War Chiefs

---

[2] In Fox the stem kīgäno- ordinarily translated "to celebrate a gens festival", etc., is used also in the sense of "to celebrate ceremonial festivals" which are unconnected with gentes.

Worship the Buffaloes", is a member of the Catamenial Society, and of the Buffalo Society Medicine Bundles.

Wi ta ka is a member of the War Chiefs gens, is a singer in "When the War Chiefs Worship the Wolf", is simply one of those seated in "When the War Chiefs Worship the Buffaloes", is a member of the Buffalo Society Medicine Bundles.

Mi da tti ne ni is a member of the War Chiefs gens, and is a singer in both "When the War Chiefs Worship the Wolf" and "When the War Chiefs Worship the Buffaloes."

Wi ka me is a member of the War Chiefs gens, and is a singer in both "When the War Chiefs Worship the Wolf" and "When the War Chiefs Worship the Buffaloes."

We ki ma A is a member of the War Chiefs gens, and is a singer in both "When the War Chiefs Worship the Wolf" and "When the War Chiefs Worship the Buffaloes."

Wa so se according to one list of Kiyana is a member of the War Chiefs gens, but according to another list of the same informant a member of the Kindly Chiefs gens. It will be recalled that I have previously explained that I do not wholly understand the interrelation of these two gentes. She is a hummer in "When the War Chiefs Worship the Wolf" and in "When the War Chiefs Worship the Buffaloes", she belongs to the organization named "When the War Chiefs Raise the Flag", and is presumably a hummer.

Na na A la me ga is a member of the War Chiefs gens, and she is a hummer in "When the War Chiefs Worship the Wolf" and "When the War Chiefs Worship the Buffaloes", and in the Catamenial Society.

Le mi ta no ga is a member of the Fish gens and she is a hummer in "When the War Chiefs Worship the Wolf"; if she belongs to other organizations, I am ignorant of it.

Le ma na gi is a member of the Thunder gens, and she is a hummer in "When the War Chiefs Worship the Wolf" and the Dirty Little Ani which belongs to the Thunder gens.

A sa wa sa mo is a member of the War Chiefs gens; the dual division to which she belongs is given by Kiyana on four separate occasions to be the Tō'kān one but by another informant (see Bull. 89, Bur. Amer. Ethn., p. 59) she is said to be a Ki'ckō. She is a hummer in "When the War Chiefs Worship the Wolf", is merely present "When the War Chiefs Worship the Buffaloes", is a member of "The War Chiefs Raise the Flag", is a hummer in the Catamenial Society, and also one in the Thunder Dance of the Bear gens.

Ne wa ki ki is stated by Kiyana on one list to be a member of the War Chiefs gens, but on another list to be a member of the Kindly Chiefs gens (cf. supra). She is a hummer in "When the War Chiefs Worship the Wolf", is merely seated "When the War Chiefs Worship the Buffaloes", is a member of "The War Chiefs Raise the Flag", and belongs to the Dirty Little Ani of the Thunder gens.

Di di ga ne sa is a member of the Bear gens; he is a singer in "When the War Chiefs Worship the Wolf", "When the War Chiefs Worship the Buffaloes", "The War Chiefs Raise the Flag", the Dirty Little Ani of the Thunder gens, the Catamenial Society; is the head ceremonial attendant in the Great Sacred Pack of the Thunder gens, is the head singer in the organization centering around the Sāgimā'kwäwA sacred pack of the Bear gens, directs the eaters in the Thunder Dance of the Bear gens, belongs to the Buffalo Dance of the Bear gens, and is a member of the Bird Dance (i. e., WâpAnōwiweni) of the Bear gens (singer, director of ceremonial attendants).

Ka we si A is a member of the Fish gens, is a singer in "When the War Chiefs Worship the Wolf", "When the War Chiefs Worship the Buffaloes", Buffalo Head Dance of the Thunder gens, the Catamenial Society, is the drummer in the Red Stone Pipe ceremony of the Eagle gens, is a member of the Buffalo Society Medicine Bundles, also of the Spotted Face Society, and also belongs to a Potawatomi buffalo dance at Tama, Iowa.

E ni ka wa is a member of the War Chiefs gens and is merely seated in both "When the War Chiefs Worship the Wolf" and "When the War Chiefs Worship the Buffaloes"; he apparently also belongs to "The War Chiefs Raise the Flag."

Le mo se A is a member of the War Chiefs gens and is merely seated "When the War Chiefs Worship the Wolf."

A no ta is a member of the War Chiefs gens and is merely seated "When the War Chiefs Worship the Wolf"; is said to belong also to "The War Chiefs Raise the Flag."

No ka wa ta is a member of the War Chiefs gens; he is twice designated by Kiyana as a Kī'ckō, though once called a Tō'kān by a younger informant, which last I consider to be an error. He is merely seated "When the War Chiefs Worship the Wolf", and "When the War Chiefs Worship the Buffaloes", is a member of "The War Chiefs Raise the Flag"; at one time he was a more or less orthodox Christian, also has been a member of the Peyote cult, and once was a member of the so-called Religion Dance.

Ma ya tti is a member of the War Chiefs gens and is merely seated "When the War Chiefs Worship the Wolf." Presumably he is a Tō'kān.

A ge A ta is a member of the War Chiefs gens; she is presumably a Kī'ckō; she is merely seated "When the War Chiefs Worship the Wolf."

In the above discussion "is" is used as a matter of convenience; some have died (see below), and other changes have taken place. And also my knowledge of the activities mentioned is deficient to the

extent that my information on these was not synchronous. In one
case a member of the Catamenial Society (whose name is withheld by
agreement) has dropped out of the organization; his little pack was
taken back; but details are lacking. Except where noted I have in-
dependent means of knowing the gentes and dual divisions given are
correct.

The account on page 93 et seq. gives the organization as it existed
only a few years ago. It will be noticed that this account partially
repeats itself. I combine them in the following:

Shawata speaker, and blows the flute.	Di di ga ne sa
Ma gi la na da A speaker after the last eating.	Wa so se A
	A sa wa sa mo
Ki dka ta li wa (Li da A) drummer.	Ne ta ko se ⎤ women who belong.
Wi di ka kya singer.	Na wa te
No ka wa ta singer.	Ne wa ki ki ⎦
Ta ta la ko A leader of songs.	

The difference in the personnel is accounted for mostly by death
(Me ne we ki ma wa, Kya na wa, Ke le yo A, A la ta o na, Ki yo sa ta
ka, We ki ma A, Ka we si A; possibly others). Other factors have
also been operative: Some members have lost general interest in
Fox ceremonials, some have taken up the Peyote rite, others have
been converted to Christianity, one, I think, has dropped out because
he is too deeply engrossed with other ceremonial organizations; one
person has been elevated from being merely a sitter to a singer because
of increased interest, and political "pull" may have helped; a new
recruit from the Bear gens has been probably added because of his
importance in Fox ceremonials in general and in Fox politics; and
changes have also occurred in accordance with the desires of the
leaders. It may be added that Na wa te is a Kï'ckō, and that according to one list she is a member of the Thunder gens but according to
another of the War Chiefs gens. I have definite knowledge that
three of her brothers belong to the Thunder gens, and one brother
(Nä nä ma kï sa) certainly has a name appropriate to the Thunder
gens ("Little Thunderer"). (For the names of her brothers see p.
211 of The Iowa Journal of History and Politics, Vol. IV, Iowa City,
Iowa, 1906.) Her father belongs to the Thunder gens, and her mother
(Ne ta ko se) to the War Chiefs gens. The name of a sister is given
there also, but I have no information regarding her gens. It may
be Na wa te belongs to such cases in which the person belongs to the
gens of his or her father, though having a name suitable to the gens
of the namer. I have touched on such cases previously. Or, it
may be that at the time of naming it was agreed that she should belong
to the gens of her namer. Besides belonging to the organization
under discussion she also belongs to "The War Chiefs Raise the Flag",
and she is a hummer in the Buffalo Head Dance of the Thunder gens.

Her ceremonial affiliations do not help us in determining her gens; I have more than once alluded to the "placing" of persons in ceremonial organizations which do not belong to the gentes of such persons; there are a few Fox ceremonial organizations which do not belong to any particular gens, but such is not the ordinary case. Ne ta ko se is a Tō'kān, belongs to the War Chiefs gens, and is a member of "The War Chiefs Raise the Flag." Ki dka ta li wa is a Tō'kān and belongs to the War Chiefs gens. He is a member of "The War Chiefs Raise the Flag", and, I think, of the Catamenial Society; he is (or was) a singer in "When the War Chiefs Worship the Buffaloes." Wi di ka kya (hypocoristic for Wi di ka kye ska ka) is merely seated in "When the War Chiefs Worship the Buffaloes", is a member of "The War Chiefs Raise the Flag", is a ceremonial attendant and head Tō'kān dancer in the Thunder Dance of the Bear gens, is a member of the organization centering around the A'penäwänä'A sacred pack of the Thunder gens; he has some connection with the Great Sacred Pack of the Thunder gens, at any rate is not supposed to eat at the appurtenant festival. Ma gi la na da A is the oldest son of PA'ci-tōnīgwA, the last chief of the Meskwakies recognized by the Federal Government. He is a Kī'ckō'A and a member of the Bear gens, is a singer in the Catamenial Society, fumigates the sacred pack in the ceremony appurtenant to the Great Sacred Pack of the Thunder gens, is a head singer in the ceremony appurtenant to the Sāgimā'-kwäwA pack of the Bear gens, is a speaker in the Bird Dance (i. e., WâpAnōwiweni) of the Bear gens, "knows the songs", directs the ceremonial attendants, is a speaker in the Thunder Dance of the Bear gens, is a prominent member of the Religion Dance, and is an all-round politician among the Meskwakies (Foxes). Further changes have now (spring 1933) taken place, but I am unfamiliar with the details save that Ta ta la ko A (John Leaf) is dead. [Da wa te is also dead. 1936.]

THE WOLF GENS

How the Green Buffalo Bestowed a Blessing, and What Happened to the One Whom He Blessed, From Childhood Upward

It is said that there were twin boys. One was born first and one was born afterward. Both were members of the Wolf gens. Their appearances indeed closely resembled each other. Their eyes were alike, and their statures were the same.

They were never told to do anything. They were loved by their mother and also by their father, indeed by all their relatives. They all loved them alike. Indeed the pair were clad in regalia by them, yet they were boys.

Then, it is said, the man was told by his fellow men, "Come, make your sons fast for a little while at least." It is said that that was what he would be told. Indeed it was not to be. "Impossible. It is not my heart's wish that I should make my children hungry in such a way", it is said that he would always reply. Finally the people took notice of him. Indeed the two were the only children he had. Always he would be told to make them fast, and always he would refuse. "No", he would indeed always reply.

And then, it is said, one of his children soon became ill. He did not become sick suddenly; he began to get sick gradually. Yet he became increasingly ill. As for his father, he went and besought one who knew much about medicine. He indeed asked him to make his son well. "I will not say, 'all right', to you. I do not know what effect this medicine of mine will have upon him. After I have found out what effect it has on him then I will tell you. I will tell you in 4 days. I will indeed tell you if he is to get well at all", the one who had the son was told. The skilled doctor indeed slept at their home. The man was worried over his son. And, it is said, when the 4 days were up he was told, "It is impossible. I can not make him well. Indeed it is very difficult. Your son indeed will succumb." When he was told that, he wailed. He wept. "Well, you may try to doctor him as long as he is alive", the skilled healer was told. "Very well", he said.

Indeed soon his patient lost strength. Soon a young man came to look at him. After the one who was doctoring went out, the man was told, "Perhaps I can make your son well. I will not say that I can certainly do so. I said, 'perhaps.' This is what is the matter with him. He is tubercular. The one who has left will not know that that is the matter with him, that he is tubercular. I am the only one who can heal those who are so afflicted. That is why I have said to you, 'perhaps I can heal him for you' ", he said to the father.

"Now you have gladdened my heart", he was told. "The one who has left will stop giving him medicine to drink", he said of the one who had been doctoring his son. It is said that when the doctor came back he was told that. "Now then, I shall again search for some one to try to doctor him", he was told. "Why, to be sure", he replied, it is said. The doctor departed. It is said that that young man doctored him. He indeed truly healed him. He healed him rapidly. The father was very glad.

It is said that he was told by the one who had cured his son, "Now you had better make your sons fast. You know how you have felt in your heart. I have indeed made your son rise. No one else made him rise for you. I have now told you to do that. That is the only way their lives will be made strong. Only this. If you do not make them fast they will always indeed get sick. They will be sickly", he was told by that one. "Now then, boy, this medicine indeed is the thing that will always make them well. There are many of you who can doctor", he was told. "Indeed I do not think at all in this way of them, that they must be made hungry", the young man insisted. "As for myself, I simply went hungry and did not have any kind of a dream", he said, and ceased to say any more to him.

Then, it is said, soon afterward the people became ill. And that man became sick and also one of his sons. His son died first and he died a little while afterward. And one of them did not become ill at all. It is said that the one who did not die commenced to fast. He was yet only a boy. He was a pretty good sized boy. He would always fast continually. It is indeed said that he even fasted during the summer. It is said that he would not take food, nor would he be tempted to eat early. And, it is said, the aged took notice of that boy and observed that he fasted earnestly after his father had left him. He now lived only with his mother.

Now it is said that once during the winter he was seen weeping. Behind him stood a buffalo. The buffalo was green. It is said that the boy did not see him at all. He did not know that the buffalo was there. It was then wintertime. After the boy had departed, one who had spied him went over to where the boy was weeping. Indeed he could not track the buffalo. That boy was the only one whom he could track. The man indeed could not even track the buffalo. "Why, it is very certain that I saw a buffalo whose fur was green", he thought in his heart. Then, it is said, he untied his Indian tobacco. He scattered it by dropping it upon the spot. He was offering a smoke to that buffalo.

He then departed. When he had come over yonder he told about it. "Why, I saw a buffalo where the twin was weeping; it was back of him. As for him, it is very likely that he did not know about the buffalo. Still, I could not track the buffalo. After he left I went over to see where his tracks led to. Indeed I could not track him", he said to those to whom he was relating this. "It is very likely that he was a manitou buffalo", he was told. "Why, it is very certain that he will be blessed by that one. Or it may be that it was himself. It is one way or the other", the old men said. "I went there and cast tobacco. I offered him a smoke unknowingly", he said. "Oh, you have done rightly. That is the reason why he has shown himself to you", he was told.

Then, it is said, later on there was a swamp in precisely the direction they were to go. Indeed it was the only direction they could go. Still, it was very difficult. Even when they threw wood there, they would gradually sink out of sight in the mud. "Why, what can this be?" they said. Then they thought of that twin. A warrior went over to speak to him. He came to where the twin was. "Why, my grandchild, a difficult task is desired of you. You will do, it is said, what is desired of you. That is what the men say. Again, our chiefs have thought of you in the same way. It is indeed said that you must try to do so", he was told. "This is what has been desired of you. It is very difficult for us to go through this swamp at the present time. It is desired that you take the people through. Indeed our chiefs have desired you to do that for them. That is the mission I have been sent on, and that is the reason I have come to you, my grandchild", the warrior said to him. As for the young man, he sat just as he had sat at first. He did not speak at any time. It is said that that was exactly what he did. Then, it is said, when that warrior started to depart, the young man asked him, "When shall I take them across?" "Why, you are to say that. Indeed exactly at the time you name we will move. You can indeed suit yourself", he was told. "I shall not say to anyone, it will be at this time. It will be for you to say it, and just as you say so, that will be the time when the people will move", he was told. "Well, it will be tomorrow at noon. Still, you ought to come here again", he said to the warrior. "You should come here very early", he said to him. "Very well", he replied.

It is said that the warrior then departed. And, it is said, the warrior returned very early in the morning, indeed it was when he had finished eating. He had already told the chiefs. "The twin has consented", he said to them. And when it was nearly noon, the young man said to him, "Now you may say to them, 'let us move.' They must be quick when they take the coverings off their houses. You must say to them, 'it has been said that you must be in haste when you take the coverings off your houses'". So the warrior was told.

"Very well", he said. He went outside. "Oh ho! it is said that we are to move. It is said that you must be in haste when you take the coverings off your houses", he said to the people. Indeed they were in haste when they took the coverings off. Indeed every one of them took their coverings off.

Then, it is said, that boy said, "A member of the War Chiefs gens must paint me. He is to paint me green." Then he was painted by a member of the War Chiefs gens. He was painted green by him all over. Indeed he was even painted green on the soles of his feet. After he was completely painted green he said to the people, "Now then, we are all to step on the same track. I am to make tracks as I go. You may indeed follow my tracks. Those who are members of the War Chiefs gens are the only ones indeed who can follow close to me, indeed all of them, as many as there are. Then when their tracks disappear any one can follow. Still, they will indeed follow my tracks in a line. Their tracks must follow mine. Let no one wish to go on the side. Indeed you must go in the same path upon which I go. Whatever path I shall take, that is what we are to use the remainder of this evening. Indeed, if someone has forgotten something, he may go back and get it. That is what I have to say to you", he said, and departed.

Then the members of the War Chiefs gens walked along in the rear. After some time they came where the solid earth was. They then camped. Others indeed were just starting to come. Then the members of the War Chiefs gens were told, "Well, you are to cook for our friends. You are indeed to build the camps", they were told. "Very well", they replied. The women then started to cook. Then the men went out to cut poles. They built camps for every one of the people. Again, after they had cooked all of them came and ate what was cooked. They did not have to say, "Eat!" to them. They simply cooked for them.

The people had now camped in safety. The next day they were forbidden to go back and try to walk on the route they had come. They were told, "Indeed, this is very terrible. You know this very well, that the sticks even sink in there. Those sticks float on the water, yet they indeed sink here. Yet I have indeed carried all of you across. Very likely something would happen to you should you turn back. It may be that we should all be killed by some people. Indeed that is what would happen to us if we did go back there. Now indeed we shall not meet any misfortune. If that had turned us back we should have been an easy prey to those who speak alien languages. That is what our fate would have been. Now it will not be that way. We shall not be easily killed. Indeed every one of us who call each other 'people' have been led or have tried to be led through something difficult. The one who goes through this will be the one who is strongest among his fellow people. Here is where every one of the people will turn back, but we indeed have already gone through this. Indeed it has ever been so. Everyone fears this. Even a little bird, even ducks, indeed all who fly fear this. Should they alight here, then they would sink down. Even if ducks should alight here they would sink down. This even would kill fish. That is what I have to tell you", he said to the people. The people were frightened for the first time. "As for the manitou or any one else, they have called this the 'War-lake.' That is the reason why these members of the War Chiefs gens were the first to follow me. As for the manitou, he does not forget the members of the War Chiefs gens. Here is where those who have been made members of the War Chiefs gens by their fellow manitous will stay. This is their lake. No one is treated gently by this. Indeed if you even throw snapping turtles in it they will indeed die here. And we all know that snapping turtles live in mud. Yet they would indeed be killed here as anything else. That is the reason why I tell you when speaking to you that I have brought you through difficulty", he said to the people.

Then he said, "We are to stay here for 8 days. Then we can move. This is the trouble with this ground. This ground has a hole in it as far as yonder. That is the reason why it is this way. That is the reason why anyone may be killed by it."

After 8 days had passed the people moved. Then, it is said, the people offered it a smoke. They all cast tobacco for it as they started to move.

"Tonight you must look backward", he said to the people. When night came then it was that they looked backward, indeed everyone. Indeed they saw fire sparkling. "This is like that every winter. It is doing so simply to show you", he said. They indeed again cast their tobacco in that direction. "This we now offer you to smoke, our grandfather", they would say. "As soon as I see my fellow man, may I slay him. That is what I ask of you", said those who sacrificed tobacco. It is indeed said that that was what every one of them said.

"Indeed you did not ask for long life. You have asked for something which is frightful. You were to have asked for something right", the young man said to them. "The manitou made it to be peaceful for us. And we did not lose each other there. We have safely crossed the hole in the earth. Because he told it to be peaceful is why we went across. If he had done what you ask, why we should indeed have all sunk in that swamp. We should not have been able to crawl out at all. Indeed it is very certain that this miry mud would kill us", he said to them.

"As it is, this one who is a member of the War Chiefs gens may tell him that. He may ask for that very thing. But as for you, you cannot. Your pleas are in vain. He is the only one to whom that manitou will listen. How can it be otherwise? He belongs to the same gens. For that manitou is declared to be a member of the War Chiefs gens by his fellow manitous. His life indeed is the same as that of the members of the War Chiefs gens: indeed he is made so that he will not treat anyone kindly. That is the reason why he will not listen to you others", the twin said.

Indeed, it is said, now the men commenced to consider him unusual. "It is very certain that he will be greatly talked about for something", they said of him. "He even knows about this place where he carried us across. Again, he even knows about the manitou who must dwell there. Indeed he knows how that manitou came to be a manitou."

It is said that from then on they were afraid of him. It is said that whenever there was a gens festival, the best food was served that boy. Moreover, when only warriors were invited he also would be invited by the one who did the inviting. It is said that whenever he was gone they would come to his dwelling and invite him. It is said that he usually sat with the leading warriors. Indeed he would always be treated like this.

And, it is said, when he was a little bigger he began to understand wolves of every kind. And his mother noticed that whenever a wolf howled he would listen very attentively to it. Sometimes he would laugh. The wolves would make him laugh. Again, her son would always tell what kind of a day was coming in the future. Indeed the days would be just so. And at a certain time when the woman and he were sitting down she said to him, "Now, my son, I have desired in my heart to know something about you. Why is it that you seem to know about the future weather?" "Oh so! This is the reason why I know. These wolves always tell what kind of a day it is to be in the future. That is why I know. When they talk about anything I understand them. It seems indeed as if it were people calling. I seem to hear them in that manner", he said to his mother. "So I have observed, my son. Whenever our grandfathers howl, I think, 'my son understands them.' Indeed it has happened that you do. That is all I am going to ask you", the woman said to her son. "I have now told you, mother", he said to her. "Well, my son, cease telling that you understand your grandfathers", he was told by his mother. Then, it is said, he was told, "What have they to do with you?" "Those wolves indeed are they who look after us. If someone comes, for example, a scout, they are the ones who would tell me of it. They would indeed tell where he is. Again, they would indeed tell when the scouts would be sound asleep.

These wolves look after us that way. That is the reason they howl so loudly at times. Sometimes they howl loudly because they ask tobacco from us, for they are in need of a smoke. Yet they obtain their smoking from here only. They are not given a smoke from elsewhere, even indeed they are not given a smoke by those whom they have blessed. And they are not given a smoke by those who speak a different language. It is us only, any of us, by whom they are given a smoke", he said to his mother.

The woman's heart was relieved. And it is said she took good care of her son. It happened that he was a handsome young man. The girls all loved the twin, but he paid no attention to them. It is said that the old woman would always forbid her son to court them. Finally the old woman was told, "It may be that you do not understand me. I have said that I shall not go courting. Still, you do not cease to tell me that. I surely would listen to anyone if he said 'Don't' to me." She then ceased to say anything further. "I must yet do much fasting", the old woman was told. "That is so", she only replied to her son.

And during that winter he fasted very earnestly. He surely fasted very earnestly. Finally he had a dream. Someone spoke to him, "Now, my grandchild, you have more than made yourself hungry. After you have grown older all the manitous will indeed know you. Still, they will not be those who are seated up above. Those who are seated underneath this earth are they who will then remember you, that is, after you have grown to be a young man. Indeed they will especially bless you. You will not be blessed with poor blessings. Indeed you will be blessed with whatever is in their power to bless. Indeed if the manitou is allowed any amount of power, indeed your blessing will be very rich. The Great Manitou has the power in his heart, and the manitous conform to this in whatever way they bestow blessings", he was told in his dream. "You had better, therefore, cease to paint yourself with charcoal. You have done your duty long ago", he dreamed he was told. "Still your blessing will only be conferred when you have grown up", he was told.

Then he told his mother, "This is what I have dreamed: It is said that I am to cease fasting. I was told in my dream, 'the manitous are thinking of you' ", he said to his mother. " 'Indeed when you have grown up you will know your blessing.' That is what I was told in my dream", he said to his mother. He ceased to fast.

Then, it is said, later on, during the summer when the people went on a buffalo hunt they also went. It is said that they went in boats when they went on the buffalo hunt. They rowed upstream. After they had gone a long distance, they started to drag their canoes up the banks. From there they all went overland. Then, it is said, he had a vision of the buffaloes, and that he was not to eat them. The young man found this out.   He told his mother, "Why, it will be improper for me to eat buffaloes any more", he said to his mother.   "Indeed I shall merely see them for you", he said to her.   And after they had indeed gone a long distance in their hunt they saw buffaloes.   The next day the men gave chase.   They ran on foot.   It is said that some jumped astride of the buffaloes and rode them as they shot them.   Indeed the men killed many buffaloes.   That young man also shot at them, but he did not like their smell.   And, it is said, the women roasted the meat on spits near the fire; and the people also roasted the meat over the fire.   They indeed prepared much buffalo meat.   Whenever they would start to waste the meat he would go off somewhere else.

After they had been on the chase four times the leader said, "Now then, let us stop killing them."   "Very well", they said to him.   Then they learned that the young man did not eat buffaloes, for he could not eat them.   They helped him as he went out to shoot some little birds or anything else.   He was to eat these little birds or whatever else he shot.

And, it is said, his mother continued to scold him.   Especially when many women were around he would be scolded as if he were a child.   Indeed the scolding which he received embarrassed him.

When they had come to where their canoes were they started to load them.   They departed.   They now went downstream.   The river was very wide.   It is said that as they paddled along one entire night they saw many canoes afloat.   They had met their foes.   After they had gone through them they paddled fast.   They seemed to be very helpless.   Then they were told by that young man, "They will not know anything of us", he said to them.   They then camped far off.   They paddled by on the other side of the stream.   It is said that some of the women even cried, for they were badly frightened.   Indeed they even went and besought him that they might live.   "Come, cease bothering me for a short time.   They will know nothing about us", he said to them.   "We have met them and they will not know we have passed them", he said to them.

And when they had moved again, he said to the people, "You will now see the one who watches over all of us.   Yet you must indeed all burn tobacco for him.   Let no one refrain from burning tobacco for him.   That is the one who blesses me.   If you give tobacco to the one who always watches us wherever we go, he will be very proud.   We have now already passed through the spot which is feared.   That is the reason you will see him", he said to them.   "I shall not say, 'Here he is.'   You will know him as he will be conspicuous.   You will then think in your hearts, 'Why, here he is' ", he said to them.   "You must look ahead", he said to them.   Indeed they always looked ahead.   Soon they saw a wolf going across their way.   The wolf was walking on top of the water.   Indeed he walked along very slowly.   Everywhere the people untied their tobacco and burned it for him in earnest. The wolf walked on ahead very slowly and unconcernedly. And just as soon as he came upon the land he howled. They saw wolves running all about them. It is said that some of them ran across the river. And some of the wolves ran along on the top of the water. "The tobacco which you have burned is now being offered. Those who were told to watch us are given an equal amount", he said to the people. "You know how many there are. Those are they who watch. They are of such a nature that they will not tell a falsehood", he said to the people.

Then, it is said, they now ceased being in any way afraid. They now ceased to think in their hearts about their enemies. They now came from where they had started. Their belongings had remained unmolested. And those who had stayed where they were living were unmolested. These were told of what had happened and they were frightened. "Very likely they may have happened to row by here during the night. Quite a while ago it rained here every night", they said. "Very likely it was during the last time that they passed by here", said one who usually kept track of affairs. "Or, it may have been that they thought we were very numerous, and so passed by in the night. As these dwellings are many in number, they must have been deceived by them", they said among themselves.

Then the twin dreamed, "You will now travel about. You must depart tommorow and exercise your legs", he was told. As soon as he awoke he went outside. He ran in no fixed direction. It happened that at first he ran toward the east. Indeed he came to find himself standing at the edge of the great sea and facing the east. He did not know from whence he had come. "You may stay here 4 days", he was told. He could not see the one who had spoken to him. "Very well", he said unknowingly. And after 4 days he was told, "You will now run toward the south." He started to run aimlessly. He again soon knew that he was standing. He was standing near the edge of the great sea. It was in the south. It was hot. Then he was indeed told, "You must remain here 4 days." He could not indeed see the one who had spoken to him. He again said unknowingly, "Very well." Then again he ran on after 4 days. And as he ran there was a path ahead of him. That, it is said, is what he would think in his heart. And he again soon knew that he was standing. And indeed just then the sun glowed red as it went down. Then indeed he was told, "You must remain here for 4 days." Unknowingly he again said, "Very well." He indeed could not see the one who had spoken to him. And after 4 days he ran on. He started to run aimlessly. And he again suddenly knew that he was standing. He could only see. He indeed was told the same thing. "You must remain here indeed for 4 days", he was told. "Very well", he thought

in his heart.   It had indeed happened that he was completely frozen.
His eyes indeed had good vision.   After 4 days there came a green
buffalo.   It spoke to him, "My grandchild, myself, your heart is also
my heart", he was told.   It is said that the buffalo took him underneath the earth.   "It is I, my grandchild, who has wished you to run
around this island", he was told.   "I am the one who has tried how
fast you are", he was told.   "Indeed nothing will be the matter with
you.   Thus, you have thought in your heart, 'I am frozen.'   I have
made you to be as my hoof.   You have never known a buffalo's hoof
to be cracked open by freezing.   My grandchild, nothing will happen
to us."   It is said that something which had befallen him ceased.   He
was no longer cold.   He now also ate.   After he had eaten some meat,
"Do you know what you are eating?" he was asked.   "I have fed you
human flesh.   I have fed you this because you are very hungry.
You are eating for your meal a chief only", he was told.   "Whenever
you go any place you will kill a chief.   That is the aim of your meal",
he was told.   He was exultant.   "You will now return.   I shall take
something to you later on", he was told by that green buffalo.   "It
will not be at the present time.   Indeed you own it.   No one else has
been so blessed.   It is your possession", he was told.   "Yet, my
grandchild, it will be only at that time when you will see it", the twin
was told.   Then he was told, "Now, my grandchild, I am going to
take you."

It was during the night.   Just as soon as they were outside he
recognized their dwelling.   He went there.   He lay down just as he
was.   The next day there were loud sounds of those who were weeping.
"The twin, the twin", they indeed said.   They mentioned him many
times.   He went outside and someone saw him.   They ceased weeping.   "Gracious!" he said to them.   He then told his mother, "Mother,
I was made to run in a circle over this earth", he said to her.   "Oh",
she replied.   "You did not finally run yourself to death?" she asked.
"I did not know what I was doing.   When I ran I ceased to know
anything for a while.   Then again, I would suddenly know when I
would be standing near the edge of the great sea.   That is what
happened to me", he said to his mother.   "Why, good gracious, it
must be that a manitou is thinking of you.   Who is it that has the
endurance to run to the shore of the great sea?   Very likely you are
blessed by one who is called a 'manitou' ", she said to her son.

Then, it is said, the people moved.   They were moving off toward
some unknown place.   After they had moved four times the leader
was killed by a deer.   It is said that then they did not know in which
direction they should move.   That deer escaped from them.   They
did not kill it.   Then that young man was wanted in order to kill
the deer.   "It's just to try, for it is not likely that I shall overtake

it", he said. He ran where it had run. In a little while he saw it running. He gave chase. After he had pursued it hotly it changed into an Indian. Lo, it is said that it was a Sioux. The young man caught him. After he had bound him securely he took him back. After he had brought him back he said to his fellow Indians, "This is that deer. It was a Sioux Indian." Thus he said to them. They then, it is said, tortured the Sioux. The young man looked on as they tortured the Sioux. Suddenly, after the Sioux was dead, a warrior came rising from his seat. "You have now made a capture, my grandchild. You have captured a manitou who had come on the warpath against us. You are to be dreaded indeed", the young man was told. He said nothing and departed. When he came to their dwelling only those who had been in severe battles came to him. He had beaten them all in courage. They started to talk to him. They told him that he had done the hardest thing. After they had told him that, he said to them, "I only went to overtake him for you. I do not wish in my heart to become a warrior." Thus the young man spoke.

"You will have full control as to where we shall have our town", he was told. "I can not consent to this. You are much older", he said to them. "I do not yet know anything in advance", he said to them. Then someone agreed to be the leader when moving. He was the one who had full control as to where their town was to be. After he selected it, he moved. The people truly camped there in safety. There was no one who was ill. Again they had plenty of meat as they went along. They killed game easily. Indeed it seemed as if the game were getting more plentiful as they moved on. They finally came to their destination. Just as soon as they had finished building their town dwellings some people who were their enemies came upon them. They then began to hold a council with those who spoke different languages. Indeed every one of them spoke different languages. They were holding a council regarding this earth, to determine who had been sent here by the manitou to own this earth. Everyone indeed said, "I." Then the Meskwakies were just sitting down. It is said that the Indians were seated in different groups, each group being composed of those who spoke the same language. And they would always take that young man. They would always tell the things the manitou had wished them to do. Then that young man said to every one of those people, "Well, though we are now holding a council here, it seems indeed as if we were holding this council secretly. Indeed no one has as yet said anything about it to the manitou. As for me, if I were to mention the manitou, I would do that which he would know." Then he was told by the people, "Come now, you may tell the manitou. Indeed, you may tell him in such a way that he will know about us." "Well, I shall do that tomorrow", he said to them. "Yet the one who is right will be then known", he said to them. "Tomorrow we shall see what kind of a sky there will be overhead. There is going to be a chieftain sky.[1] Again, a chieftain's fire will be flaming. From there indeed we shall light our pipes. I have now spoken. When I talk about this earth of ours I shall be right. I shall be the one to speak especially rightly. Still, you who speak these different languages must now speak. I shall speak the last", he said to them.

The next day when they woke up the sky was entirely green. Again the fire was very large and was burning a green flame. There was no wood there at all. They only saw the fire. And they held a council there. That young man started to talk to the men. After they had all gathered they began to talk. And that young man indeed spoke the last. "Now, my friends, the manitou also knows me. He has made me to stand on top of this earth. He has made me the owner of the things on and under this earth. And he has not lent them to me. I am the owner. That is why I can say 'I am the owner'", he said to the people. It is said that they all were then very angry. And the people began shooting in lively fashion. Then he told them to loosen the ground around the fireplace. Also he told them that no one should spit in it. He told this to a messenger. It is said that the messenger ran on giving instructions. He was not shot while going about giving instructions. After he had finished telling them and after they had fixed their fires, their fires suddenly indeed burned a green flame. As for those who were shooting at them, they suddenly lost those at whom they were shooting. Those dwellings had sunk down into the earth. And where the dwellings had stood there now remained only red earth. Indeed where the dwellings had stood the earth was in the form of paint. Surely those people were then frightened. "Why, those people must be manitous", the people said. They soon feared it and all moved away. They moved off to some unknown spot.

Then after 4 years the dwellings which had sunk came up. Then, it is said, he was told, "Well, you must go after something." He was told that plainly and did not dream it. He indeed started off aimlessly. Suddenly he saw someone standing in the middle of a hill. He saw the being was large. He was in no way afraid of it. He went over to where it was. When he came close, lo! it was a large buffalo. It was very large. Indeed it was of an enormous size. When he was yet some distance from it the buffalo began to diminish in size. It had a green coat of fur. When the young man came on the spot, lo! there remained the good-sized hide of a young buffalo. It indeed had green fur. That was what he had beheld as a buffalo.

---

[1] I. e., the sky will be clear and green, for green is the color (paint) of the Bear gens, in the Black Bear division of which the chieftainship is supposed to be hereditary.

He picked it up. When he picked it up it shot out little sparks of fire. Nevertheless he picked it up and carried it with him. Underneath it was painted red. Then he thought of placing it far off. "No, you must take it with you", he was told. He indeed took it with him to where they lived. When he had brought it there he wrapped it up carefully and put it away carefully.

Then, it is said, the people became ill. Yet they did not think of coming to the young man to have him doctor them. It is said that the people would desert the sick. Just as he fell sick the people were moving. So he and his belongings were deserted. His mother had already died among the first. It is said that the reason he was deserted was so that no one might worry over him. And, it is said, later he was able to be up. It is said that he lay sick there for a long time. And he was brought food to eat by the wolves. Those people now thought of him after they had ceased to become ill, and when all were well. They indeed all lamented him. It is said that he was now told by his buffalo hide, "Well, let me take you on. You are to have me as your sacred pack." So he was told. Then there stood a buffalo. "Now, my grandchild, get on top. I shall carry you on my back", it said to him. The young man rode it. After he had seated himself comfortably, the buffalo began to run slowly at first. Indeed his grandfather was fast. As they went he could see the people who had died. It is said that at the time the people were dying they would die from sneezing. Indeed, it is said, whenever anyone began sneezing he would be at it constantly. He then would die. That is what happened to them.

And, it is said, he overtook them in the night. "You must go forward and sleep", he was told by his grandfather who was carrying him. "They are going that way", he was told. "Whenever they see you they will camp", he was told. "Every one of them indeed is wailing for you", he was told. He then, it is said, slept very soundly. While sleeping soundly he was awakened. Lo! all around there were many people. They indeed camped there. They were very glad.

He no longer had any mother. He stayed in a chief's dwelling. It is said that he always felt lonely in his heart. "Now I have ceased to have a mother", he thought in his heart. Indeed he could not forget it in his heart.

They lived there permanently. Finally indeed he began to sleep far off. Whenever he slept there, it would be known because usually the wolves howled very loudly. In that way those with whom he was staying would know it. Those with whom he was staying loved him. Still, it was his mother whom he desired. Soon, it is said, the one who had blessed him said to him, "Why, I have blessed you justly. Come, your heart's desire is very difficult. You will see your mother", he was told by a wolf. "If you should do the same as we, she would live a long life, that is, if you wish that in your heart. She also will be told the same thing. We should indeed stay right here for 4 days", he was told by the wolves. There was nothing to stop him. "I shall do whatever you tell me to", he replied. "That is right", he was told by those wolves.

It is said that just as they were on the point of instructing him further the buffalo came by whom he had been blessed. "Now, my grandchild, you must go to the other side of the hill. There you will see your mother. You then will take her. These wolves would have told you something vulgar. But I do not say anything vulgar. 'This is what you must do to her', you would have been told. But I am not going to say anything to you. I have simply told you that you were to see her and to take her to the wickiup", he was told. He was glad. He departed for the place. Lo! there was his mother sitting down. He ran toward her and kissed her. "Oh! Mother!" he said to her. He was treated by her the same way. She kissed him repeatedly. Then they departed, and went to the wickiup. He now had a mother. Moreover, they were given materials by all with which they could build a wickiup. Again, they were given things to use when cooking. Everyone on all sides also gave them food to eat. And when they had a wickiup by themsleves he was suddenly awakened. When he awoke it was late at night. It was the fire, it is said, that woke him up. After he was awakened by it he was told, "Now you must listen closely to me. I am going to tell you exactly what the Green Buffalo ordered me to", the fire said to him. "I am now indeed going to begin telling you these songs. You must indeed catch on to how I sing them", it said to him. "Very well", he replied. The fire started to sing. After it had sung, he was told, "You must catch on." Indeed he tried strongly to catch on to as many songs as the fire had used. He knew them. Then he knew the speech which the fire had given.

"Tomorrow the Rock-Man will talk to you", he was told. "If I have made a mistake in any way, he will tell you", he was told by the fire. "That is all", it said to him.

The next day he departed. Suddenly someone called him from the other side of the hill. He went over there. Lo! there was a large boulder in the middle of a ravine. "This is the place that was selected for you", he was told. He began to be given instructions. "The way the Green Buffalo has blessed you is not easy. He desires that you will not end here. We two only have been named to keep track of your songs. That is another thing we were told to do. We are to continue to carefully sing them to you. Now, if I make a mistake you will hear and know it", he was told. That rock began to talk of the songs. That rock told in every detail exactly what the fire had told him previously. "As for myself, I shall never end as a being. As for that fire, you will always continue to use it as long as you live. You will be using it indeed at yonder time when your life will end. You cannot leave it before. Indeed the same will happen to me. Indeed it seems to me as though I were going along with you all", that rock said to him. It started to sing the gens festival songs. Indeed the rock sang them just as the fire had sung them. It sung them just the same. Then it started to give a speech. It was indeed just the same speech. It was given exactly the same way as he had been told it previously.

"That is the way I appoint it for you. Wherein have I told you falsely? Those are the same speeches to which you have listened. And the songs which you have heard are the very same."

"I think in my heart that no one has told me falsely in any way. It must be that both of your lives are right. Indeed that must be the reason why you did not mix some falsehood with this", the young man said.

"Well, we are indeed righteous. That is why we are ordered to do these things", the other said.

Then after the young man had been instructed he was also told, "You must not start to use these songs at once. It will be indeed some time from now. That is the desire of your grandfather. You will not forget these. Indeed you will know them whenever you begin to celebrate gens festivals", he was told. "This desire is only heaped upon you gradually. It has not been desired to heap it upon you all of a sudden", he was told. "Gradually it will continue to strongly affect you." And after he had been instructed he departed and went to where they lived.

He indeed already knew the gens festival songs. And later on during early spring his mother was boiling sap for sugar, and after they had cut wood he went walking about. The sun's rays were splendid and the wind was blowing quite hard. The young man was lying on his back looking at the trees. "Why, these are very strange" he thought in his heart. The trees spoke to him, "Oh, our grandchild, cease looking at us, for we are courting", they said to him. "We also are making our offspring", they said to him.

He then must have fallen asleep. Indeed just as soon as he was asleep he saw his grandfather, the Green Buffalo. He was taken by the latter. "You must go and see the house of blessings", he was told by that buffalo. "Very well", he said to it. They went there. It is said that there were four doors in the dwelling. One faced the east, one faced the south. Bearskins were the door-flaps. And the door on the west had a flap of deerskin. And the door to which he had been taken had a raccoon skin for a flap. And he was told in his dream, "This is where you are to sit." There was a little rise of earth where he was placed. Then a man came in. He came in from the south door. Then another came in from the west side. It was a man. It is said that they did not look at the young man. Then another came from the north side. There were now four of them.

And the one who blessed him began to talk. "Now, men, I have brought our grandchild here. That is the relationship we have been given toward the people. The one who has seated us all around has told us that. The reason I have blessed him is because he fasted. I have done so because I knew he was more than in despair over the death of his brother, his fellow twin, and also his father. That is the reason why I have blessed him. I am indeed going to give him myself. That is the reason why I have wished this in my heart. I have given him myself. Indeed I have also given him my own songs", he said to them. "That is what I have to tell you", the men were told.

Then one of them began to speak. "I also wish the same for our grandchild", he said. "As for me, I am going to wish in my heart that he may have a good life. That he may live on to the full span of his life is what I wish for our grandchild." Then another spoke to him. "Indeed I also will wish the same thing for our grandchild. I shall wish for him only that which is right. Again, that disease may not enter his chief's town is what I wish for him. Again, I wish that whoever from without ever speaks evilly against their town may cease to do so. It will be even more as regards one who is constantly doing so. Indeed whoever does so will instead curse himself. That is what I shall wish for him. Again, I shall remember all who belong to the gens of which he is a member. That is what I shall wish for our grandchild", he said.

Then the fourth time he was spoken to by the buffalo who sat in the north end. "I also will bless our grandchild. I shall merely wish him this indeed. That he be considered a man is what I shall wish for him. And also this, that he may associate with all until old age. That is what I shall wish. That they never be smitten by disease is also what I wish for him. And I shall place last for him this, namely, what we consider in our hearts as 'one slice.' I wish to give him this in return for his kettleful (of offerings). That is what I wish for the one who continues to think often of our blessing. He is the one I shall especially remember. The present time will not be as far as I shall think of him. I shall think of him until this earth ceases to be an earth. That is how long I shall wish that for our grandchild.

"Again, we must be quick to hear these gens festival songs which they are to have. They must tell each other to be in earnest in thinking about them. That is what he must tell his fellow clansmen. Indeed he must tell them this in a straightforward manner. He must think in his heart to never forget this which we have wished for him. Indeed he must also tell this as a message to those who are to listen to him. Those who listen attentively to him are they who will be remembered. That is what I wish our grandchild", he said.

"Yet, men, if there are to be only as many as we are, our words will not come true. You must go yonder and summon the Great Manitou so that you may tell him how we have blessed this mortal. Our wish for him does not end at the present time. When we wish him to live until yonder time where old age is, our wish is indeed difficult. We have wished to see our wishes continue yonder to where old age is and lie about for a little while. Then the Great Manitou must come and see the one who made us sorrowful (i. e., our grandchild). And also if he is to talk he must say what he thinks of him. Indeed it will be all right if he only knows about him."

Then the Great Manitou came. The Green Buffalo informed him, "Now then, this our grandchild has made us sorrowful. He first made me to be sorrowful. Indeed these men who are here have already extended their wishes to him. No one has wished that which is wrong. We alike wished him what is right", the green buffalo said to the Great Manitou.

"Indeed I shall wish the same for our grandchild. That is the reason why I have always told you to bless our grandchildren. You have pleased me in blessing him. I too will place my blessing with yours. This is what I shall wish him. I shall only wish that which is peaceable. I shall not wish him that which is frightful. I shall only wish him that he live a good life. Indeed my wish for our grandchild is only a good quiet life. Why I have blessed our grandchild is because in that way I shall always be able to obtain a smoke from him. I wish that disease shall not strike him, and that his chief's village be not stricken with disease. That is what I wish him.

"You have pleased me in holding a council over our grandchild. You have believed me when I told you to bless the people, and have so pleased me. And now you have come to a decision over our grandchild. Indeed whatever your wishes have been they will be valid. But you must not think of taking back from him what you have wished him. Indeed you have already given him your wishes. I too have given him my wish. I shall not take it back and think about what I have wished him. Why, I have already given it to him.

"The reason I have said to you, 'be careful', is that you are not to think of conferring this blessing on simply anyone. If you should think in your hearts, 'this one is probably living rightly', he is the one whom you should bless. And the one who fasts, the one who fasts earnestly is the one whom you should continue to bless. That is what you should do with regard to our grandchildren. Now this one has truly fasted earnestly. Again, he surely has been in despair

when his father and brother died. Surely you have blessed him
justly. I am indeed of such a nature that I shall not wish anything
evil for anyone. I should bless anyone in the way I have done", he
said. He then, it is said, departed, speaking for the last time. "Tell
him how those who are to dance shall dance. And this. Tell him
the speech which we have hung (i. e., spoken)", he said. "When we
say, 'So be it', I shall remind you", he said to the young men and
the Great Manitou departed.

Then the buffaloes began to instruct the young man. "This is
how you must make the people dance. You must dance in a circle.
Again, sweet food must indeed be eaten first. That indeed is what
we will regard highly when receiving it from you, maple sirup, and
maple cakes. Also pumpkins. These are things of which we shall
think highly.

"You must always indeed worship in earnest. Do not think of anything else. You must think in your hearts of worship for 1 day.
That is what you must do. Do not think uselessly of yourselves or
friends. Indeed it seems as if you would have to put woman away for
a short time. Indeed all that you must think of for 1 day is this.
The next day you may think about the one whom you had put away.
In that way you would conduct your life rightly. That worship is
the only kind that is right. Indeed if you do not do this, you yourself
will ruin your sacred pack. Again, you will ruin your worship. There
will be no one who will think about your worship. You must forbid
your fellow clansmen to act lustfully toward each other and to look at
each other in a flirtatious way, and to jest with anyone. Indeed they
must talk quietly to one for a while at least. That is what you must
tell them. And if one has many jesting words within him, he will
make his life wretched. Indeed if even a woman should do so the
same would befall her. She would make her life wretched. She
would not bring the blame on someone else: it will be herself", he
dreamed he was told.

He awoke. When he awoke the sun was hanging just where it was
when he fell asleep. The limbs of the trees were thick. There were
many flowers. He indeed woke up in the midst of flowers. Indeed
they smelt fragrantly to him. His sleep had made him drowzy.

He now had within him those blessings. He then departed to
where his mother was staying and boiling maple sap. The dwelling
had disappeared. Then he went to where they formerly had lived.
That was gone. Then he noticed that bones were lying around where
they had had their town. The bones were bones of human dead. He
departed aimlessly. And a wolf came to him that night. "They
have had a fight. Those bones which you have seen are the bones of
your enemies. Your friends were not killed. But you have been lost.
They did not know what had happened to you. They considered

you dead", he was told. "You have been asleep for 4 years. It has now been 4 years", he was told by that wolf.

He could just now begin to feel hunger. His desire was for some sweet corn together with beans. Then that wolf said to him, "Why, I could go and tell your mother." "Well, you might speak to her with difficulty", he said to it. "She might come at full speed." "Well, that is so", said that wolf. Now the young man gave out traveling on foot. "Now then, I shall take you. I shall use medicine so that you will be strong", that wolf said. And he was given medicine. He ate it. As soon as he had eaten it he was as he had been. He was able to travel. They went on. "Perhaps we shall have to sleep 4 days on the way", the wolf said. "Very well", he replied. Indeed they walked on slowly. The young man had indeed ceased to desire the sweet corn cooked with beans. And after 4 days they came there and he was led to where his mother was. Lo! Here sat his mother with blackened cheeks. "Mother, what has been the matter with you", he said to her. "Oh! It is my son", she said to him. His mother ran toward him. The young man was petted. He then told her what he desired to eat, sweet corn cooked with beans. Shortly after nightfall the food was cooked. Then his mother questioned him. "I must have been asleep", he said to her. "The manitous verily have told me what they wish for me and how I am to conduct my gens festivals. I have been told how I must think of my gens festival. So therefore we had better build a large dwelling, mother. Soon I shall try to have the people dance", he said to his mother. "Do not go about saying this in the future, mother", he said to his mother. "It cannot be that I will go about talking about it", he was told.

Then he began to look for good upright posts. He found them that evening. They were just the way he desired them to be. And he again went out the next day. He saw some also that evening. Indeed he always did so. He would find some more every evening. On the fourth day he had found the desired number of posts. Then he went and chopped down those which he had found at first. He kept on chopping them down for 4 days. That is what he did. It took him 4 days to chop down one kind. It took him 16 days to do all the chopping. Later on he prepared them all. It is said that they were cedars. And his mother helped him. She indeed cut the poles. It is said that they would work on those green trees for 4 days. Even if the trees had large trunks it took them just that length of time. They had been told by the manitou to do this, and that was the reason they did so. Then the young man thought in his heart, "What must I do to carry these?" He had cut the trees down here and there. Then he thought in his heart, "Why, the manitou has really blessed me." He went to where they lived. When he came there he lay down to sleep. And he thought in his heart as he was lying down, "If indeed the manitou really knows me, those poles on which I worked so hard to cut down will come over here." Sure enough those poles were lying there the next morning. Then indeed he began to implant them in the ground. And the men began to help him. They thought something of him. The women also helped. In a little while they had made a large dwelling.

"Now you may summon a young man who is a member of the War Chiefs gens", he said to them. He was summoned and came. "Now, my friend, what I am going to say to you is somewhat of a nuisance. You are to walk about as a ceremonial attendant. You must go about and summon only my fellow clansmen. Indeed every one of them must come here", the youth was told. "Very well", he indeed replied. Then he was told, "You also must come here." "Very well", he replied. He departed summoning them. "You are to go to the twin's dwelling", he would say to them. He would call women or any members.

They had now gathered together. As for the ceremonial attendant, he was the only one who did not belong to that gens. The twin started to speak. "Now, men and women, children, girls, today this our ceremonial attendant has gone about summoning you to come to where I dwell. This is the reason why we are gathered here. We shall try to hunt. We are to give a gens festival. That is why we have gathered here. In 8 days you should gather and bring here by noon something. If you have anything you should bring it, sweet food or anything. We are going to worship the manitous who bless us", he said to those who were seated about him. "Still, this member of the War Chiefs gens is the one who is to act as our ceremonial attendant always. It shall not be anyone else. Indeed we shall always have this member of the War Chiefs gens to be our ceremonial attendant. Do not think in your hearts of ever changing this rule. This is the one whose services we shall always continue to ask. This one has been made by the manitou to touch the surface of the earth. He was one of the first. Again, he was the first to be made to see all things—the sun, and this sky, and the stars. That is the reason why he will act as our ceremonial attendant, this one who is a member of the War Chiefs gens. The manitou has given us members of the Wolf gens all that remain under this earth. There are many things under this earth. It has been decided that we should own those things. Whenever we imitate (?) something it will be exactly that way. The manitou has desired that we should always tell the truth. That is what I want to tell you", he said to them.

They then departed to their homes. Then, it is said, some indeed moved off. They were hunting. Indeed every one of them obeyed. And when the appointed time had come, they began bringing in the wherewith to celebrate a gens festival. Indeed there was all sorts of fresh meat—prairie chickens, quails, pheasants, squirrels, and deer meat, a bear, and harvest-crop food. And they brought in maple-sugar cakes, and maple sirup, and corn dumplings. There indeed was abundant food. And the youth acted as the leading ceremonial attendant.

After the youth had come, he was told, "Now ceremonial attendant, you may now go and get anyone whom you wish to have act as your fellow ceremonial attendants. For you are to be the leading ceremonial attendant. You indeed will only have to stay around here tomorrow. You will smoke our sacred pack", he was told. "That is all you will have to do", he was told. "Very well", he replied. Then he went around summoning those who were to act as ceremonial attendants. He went about summoning many. And it was getting to be evening when they came for their duty. They plucked the feathers off the pheasants and quail, indeed all the game. They singed the hairs off the squirrels. A little later on, the one who was to give the invitations was summoned. "Now, member of the Feathered gens, you may go and give invitations", he was told. "Very well", he replied. He then went out to invite the people. "You may invite anyone, women and also men", he was told. "Again you may also invite girls". "I shall do so", he replied. "And you, ceremonial attendant, you go directly from your dwelling and summon those who are to give the gens festival. Go out as soon as you awake. You must say to the men, 'You are to go over early to sing.' And you are to say to the women, 'Indeed you are to go over early and sit at your places.' You do not need to first come here", he was told. "Very well", he replied.

He went home. He told his parents what he had been told. "Then indeed you must wake up early", his father said to him. "You may depart from here before you have eaten," he was told. He straightway went to bed and woke up early. He departed calling those who were to give the gens festival. "Indeed you must go early to sing", he said to the men. And he said to the women, "You must go over very early and sit at your places there."

Surely after it was daybreak he went about, eating heartily. Exactly a little after sunrise he had summoned all who were to give the gens festival. He then went over to where the gens festival was to be held. And he went after some earth. He put loose earth around the fires. After bringing it, he was told, "Now, ceremonial attendant, you may spread this out", he was told, and was given a matting. "Now you are to make a mound of earth. And you may stick my feathers on top", he was told. After making the little mound of loose earth, he stuck the feathers on it. After sticking them upright he then placed the sacred pack on it. "You may also tie up the drum", he was told. "One man is to be a member of the

Feathered gens, one of the Bear gens, one of the Eagle gens, and one of the War Chiefs gens", he was told. After they had tied it up, then they placed some Indian tobacco in a pile on the middle of the drum. Then the attendants had already placed the game in the kettles to cook.

After the attendants had everything boiling, the one blessed jumped down and said to them, "Now men, you may listen to me. Eventually I am going to try to speak to our grandfathers. Verily you must catch on how I speak", he said to them. "I do not say this to one; I spoke to every one of you when I told you to catch on to what I was about to say. I have been told by the manitou to tell you this. I have indeed told you that", he said to them, and he began to give his speech.

"Now, so be it, our grandfather, so be it, you have been told this, so be it, by your fellow manitous, namely, that you were to be here, so be it, where, so be it, you could watch over us, so be it. You, so be it, are the first beings, so be it, to whom we scatter our tobacco. You are to tell correctly, so be it, in which way we extend our tobacco, so be it. You, so be it, have been named, so be it, as they who shall not fail, so be it, to utter, so be it, our wants to your fellow manitous, so be it. First of all, so be it, we remember the Green Buffalo, so be it. He, so be it, is the one to whom we first raise our hands, so be it. We extend to him, so be it, our cooked food, so be it, and also, so be it, this sweet food. Now, so be it, he was the one, so be it, who spoke to me first, so be it. So be it, he has, so be it, mentioned life to me, so be it, and what he wished me. Also, so be it, he has wished me, so be it, pleasant association with my fellow people, so be it. And he will think this, so be it, collectively, so be it, because of our tobacco. He must bless us, so be it, who belong to this one gens, so be it, in that way, so be it. You must tell him this, so be it, for us, so be it.

"Again, so be it, you must tell, so be it, the one who sits yonder, so be it, under the earth, so be it, and who sits, so be it, in the east, so be it. You also, so be it, must tell, so be it, him the same thing for us, so be it. Therefore, so be it, we speak to him in the same way so that he will wish the same for us because of our tobacco, so be it. That we may, so be it, associate with our people, so be it, till old age, so be it, is what, so be it, we say to him, so be it. That is what, so be it, you must tell him, so be it, for us, so be it. And that we shall not, so be it, have weak lives, so be it, in any way, so be it.

"Then again, so be it, we ask, so be it, from the Sunny Buffalo who dwells in the south, so be it, under the earth, so be it, the same thing, so be it. May our children, so be it, continue to live in good health. He must wish them this for us, so be it. That is our prayer, so be it, to him, so be it. That, so be it, is what you are to tell him for us, so be it, who are now made to use, so be it, this wolf name (i. e., those who belong to the Wolf gens), so be it. That he think intently of us, so be it, is what we ask you, so be it, to tell him for us, so be it.

"Then again, so be it, the Buffalo who sits yonder, so be it, straight toward the west, so be it, is also, so be it, one to whom we raise our hands. O our grandfather, you must wish that our lives reach old age because of the tobacco we have given. That is what we say to him. That is what you must say for us, our grandfather, so be it. These, so be it, who sit with me, so be it, are they to whom the tobacco belongs.

"Then again, so be it, the Northern Buffalo, so be it, who sits yonder, so be it, in the north, so be it, under the earth, so be it. That indeed is what you must tell him for us, so be it. We ask the same thing from him, so be it. He must wish, so be it, life for every one of us who belong to this one gens. We implore him that it strengthen our lives, so be it. That is what we pray as we now raise our hands toward the manitous who dwell beneath, so be it, this earth.

"We have now, so be it, named them, so be it, in a circle, so be it. And, so be it, we are all to plead with them, so be it. These pleading, so be it, all belong, so be it, to this town of ours, so be it. That our lives, so be it, will not be weak in any way, so be it, is what we ask. And may our town be well. And again, so be it, if evil disease stands about, may our dwellings stand unmolested. And may no one be afflicted with disease, so be it. And again, so be it, may whoever from without goes about speaking evilly against our town, may his desire end prematurely. May he cease to think evilly against us. That is, so be it, what we say to them, so be it. And, so be it, if he does not, so be it, cease thinking against us, so be it, may he at last, so be it, demolish, so be it, his own town, so be it. And again, we also ask, so be it, especially, so be it, from them that which was wished me last and which was placed last, one slice. May they give us life in exchange for our kettleful (of food). These are our fervent prayers we ask because of our cooked food. That is what you must carefully, so be it, tell for us, so be it, our grandfather, so be it.

"And again, so be it, we beseech, so be it, The One Who Sits In The Smoke-Hole, so be it, the same way, so be it. Oh, moreover, so be it, may you (pl.) bless us, so be it, that our heart be with your heart, so be it. That, so be it, is what we beseech of you, so be it. And, so be it, may your heart be with our heart because of our cooked food, so be it. That, so be it, is what we beseech you, so be it. That verily, so be it, you will uprightly tell, so be it, the manitous, so be it, whom we worship. How can it be, so be it, that they will not hear our prayers? How can it be, so be it, that they will turn their heads from us, so be it? Indeed, so be it, you, Spirit of Fire, so be it, our grandfather, so be it, must insist on them hearing our prayers, so be it."

That, it is said, is what the speaker said in his talk.

Then he said to his fellow clansmen, "Now, this speech is indeed very difficult. Indeed if anyone utters this from his mouth he indeed thereby obtains life. Again, if anyone knows the songs, the same will happen to him. Because our grandfather has shortened our lives too much, he has granted us to worship 1 day. We must be gentle whenever we worship. That is what the manitou expects of us. We must put aside for a short time our lustful manhood. Again, we must also put aside our funny sayings. Indeed we are only to think quietly of the manitou, and of him alone. That is what he expects us to do. Verily the one who does that is he who will be successful in his prayers. He is the one who will be remembered by the manitou. For he will be living as the manitou desired. Verily how could it be that he would not be remembered by the manitou? Indeed the manitou will remember him.

"We do not worship him long. It is just as long as these ceremonies are being performed. That is how long he must be thought of. That is why the manitou is here who knows (every) inner thought. He is seated here where he can not but know what we think in our hearts.

"And, it is said, this Spirit of Fire does not misutter our prayers to those whom we worship. He speaks, it is said, all the languages which the manitous speak. We see this Fire plainly. He cannot be held by anyone. We who are mortals fear him. Still, we will not cease to take care of him. Indeed every one of us must continue to take care of him. That is what we must do. Indeed he is the one who will look after that which we are to eat. It is not only here when we are celebrating our gens festival. It is anywhere. He helps every one of us. It is only after he has chewed our food that we can eat it. He has been told to do that. As many of us whose heads are covered with hair will use this Fire that way", he said to his fellow clansmen.

"Now then, at last we are to begin singing. We shall not continue to sing very long", he said to them. He then sang:

When I arise here;
When I arise here;
When I arise here;
When I arise here, I;
When I arise here;
When I arise here, I;
Upon this earth, my horns are fixed;
When I arise here;
When I arise here;
When I arise here, I;
When I arise here;
When I arise here;
When I arise here, I.

[A yo gi se   wa na ki ya ni;
A yo gi se   wa na ki ya ni;
A yo gi si   wa naki ya ni;
A yo gi si   wa na ki ya ne   ni na;
A yo gi si   wa na ki ya ni;
A yo gi se   wa na ki ya ne   ni na;
Ma ni   ki wi na na i wi ne;
A yo gi si   wa na ki ya ni;
A yo gi si   wa na ki ya ni;
A yo gi si   wa na ki ya ne   ni na;
A yo gi si   wa na ki ya ni;
A yo gi si   wa na ki ya ni;
A yo gi si   wa na ki ya ne   ni na.][2]

The Buffaloes here tell me, "I fear you", yes;
They fear me;
[Repeat seven times.]

[Ne di we ne me ne   ne te ko ki   A yo ko   ne no so ke   ee;
ne di we ne me ko ki;]
[Repeat, with slight variations, seven times.][3]

This is why I have spoken, so I may be quoted;
[Repeat five times.][4]

[Ma ni   we to we ya ni   wi ka wi di ke   yo   ni na;]
[Repeat five times.]

The buffaloes here call me "the Green Buffalo";
The buffaloes here call me "the Green Buffalo";
The buffaloes here;
Sacrifice a dog to me;
The buffaloes here call me "the Green Buffalo";
The buffaloes here;
The buffaloes here.

[A ski la ki ne no swa   ne te ko ki   A yo ko   ne no so ki;
A ska ki ne no swa   ne te ko ki   A yo ko   ne no so ke;
A yo ko ne no so ke;
Wa te na ma wi ko   A ne mo A;
A yo ko   ne no so ke   ski la ki ne no so   ne te ko ki;
A yo ko   ne no so ke;
A yo ko   ne no so ke.][5]

They were to dance again. "We are now going to make you dance again, our leaders", the member of the Feathered gens was told. "You must invite your woman who is to follow you", he was told. "Very well", he replied. He said to the woman, "Now then." They

---

[2] The meaning is "as soon as the young man was blessed he went to war."

[3] The buffaloes say the young man is brave. Grammatically the song should mean something very different, but two Indians (including the author) take it in the way given above.

[4] The young was blessed by the manitous so that he might slay his foes.

[5] The Chief Green Buffalo who conferred the blessing is supposed to be speaking.

went and stood in position where the sacred pack was. This dancing song was sung:

I make it dance for you, I make it dance for you;
My father, I make it dance for you, I make it dance for you, I make it dance for you;
My father, I make it dance for you, I make it dance for you, I make it dance for you;
My father, I make it dance here by the fireside, I make it dance for you, I make it dance for you;
My father, I make it dance for you, I make it dance for you, I make it dance for you;
My father, I make it dance for you, I make it dance for you, I make it dance for you.

[Ni i mi to na ni   na ni i mi to na ni;
A no se   ni na   ni i mi to na ni   na ni i mi to na ni   na ni i mi to na ni;
A no se   ni na   ni i mi to na ni   na ni i mi to na ni   na ni i mi to na ni;
A no se   ni na   yo   na na ko te ki   na ni i mi to na ni   na ni i mi to ta na ni   na ni i mi to na ni;
A no se   ni i mi to na ni   na ni i mi to na ni   na ni i mi to na ni;
A no se   ni na   ni i mi to na ni   na ni i mi to na ni   na ni i mi to na ni.] [6]

They, my fellow buffaloes, refer to me;
[Repeat three times.]
In the wilderness my fellow buffaloes (refer to) me;
They, my fellow buffaloes, refer to me.

[Wi nwa wa A   ne te ko ke   ni tti ne no so ke   ni na;
[Repeat three times.]
Na na we ka mi ke   ni tti ne no so ke   ni na;
Wi nwa wa A   ne te ko ke   ni tti ne no so ke   ni na.] [7]

Father, I speak to you from afar;
Father, I speak to you from afar, do I;
I speak to you from afar;
Father, I speak to you from afar, do I;
Father, I speak to you from afar, do I;
I speak to you from afar;
Father, I speak to you from afar, do I;
Father, I speak to you from afar;
Father, I speak to you from afar, do I;
I speak to you from afar;
Father, I speak to you from afar.

[No se   ke we to we e ne;
No se   ke we to we e ne   ni na;
Ke we to we to we e ne;
No se   ke we to we e ne   ni na;
No se   ke we to we e ne   ni na;
Ke we to we e;

---

[6] The one blessed dances around the fireside, thus showing his blessing is valid.

[7] The Green Buffalo says. "My fellow buffaloes have aided me in blessing the one I blessed, so that he may slay his foes far off and in lonely places."

No   ke we to we e ne   ni na;
No se   ke we to we e ne;
No se   ke we to we e ne   ni na;
Ke we to we e ne;
No se   ke we to we e ne.] [8]

He is instructed, he is instructed;
He is instructed, he is instructed;
He is instructed, he is instructed;
He is instructed, he is instructed, is he;
He is instructed, he is instructed, is he;
He is instructed, he is instructed.

[Na na i me ga   na ʌ na i me ga;
Na na i me ga   na ʌ na i me ga;
Na na i me ga   na ʌ na i me ga;
Na na i me ga   na ʌ na i me ga   wi na;
Na na i me ga   na ʌ na i me ga   wi;
Na na i me ga   na ʌ na i me ga.] [9]

They had now danced. "These are the songs which we are always to use. Verily I wished that you take these songs on and on. The manitou has desired that I take these songs on as long as there shall be an earth. You had better do so, my fellow clansmen", he said to them. Then he began to tell them to partake of sugar, maple cakes, sirup, the sweet foods of any kind. And after those whom he had told to partake of the food had gone out and invited others, he began to give a speech: "These are indeed that which, so be it, we first hand to the manitou, so be it, those buffaloes, so be it, who dwell, so be it, who sit fixedly, so be it, under the earth, so be it. They themselves, so be it, have already said, so be it, that they would think highly of this, so be it, that flows, so be it, from the trees, so be it. We desire, so be it, life from them, so be it, in return, so be it, for our tobacco, so be it, which we have given. We first, so be it, mention, so be it, the Buffalo, so be it, who sits permanently yonder, so be it, in the east, so be it. Again, so be it, the Sunny Buffalo, so be it, who sits permanently yonder in the south, so be it, is also, so be it, one to whom we hand this, so be it. And again, so be it, the Buffalo, so be it, who sits in the west, so be it, indeed, so be it, is one to whom we say the same when we mention them collectively, 'Pray, so be it, think of us in return for our tobacco and this sweet food.' That is what we say to them. And again, so be it, that indeed is what we say to Wintry Buffalo, so be it, who sits in the north, so be it. He must wish us good health, so be it, in return, so be it (for our offerings). That is why we have handed him, so be it, our tobacco, so be it. And therefore, so be it, you should have good health.

---

[8] The esoteric meaning assigned this song seems out of place. The Green Buffalo says, "You know how I have blessed you."

[9] The one blessed is told by the buffaloes that they have completed their instructions.

Wherefore you should eat. Eat, women and men", he said to them. That is what he said in his speech.

"Now this is the way you must speak at this time, that is, when eating the sweet food. And you also must try hard to catch on to this other one after they have eaten", he said to them.

After they had eaten he said to them, "Sit down where you were seated." Then he said, "Our chief must come here." Then he told the chief to serve the meat food. The chief then gave invitations. He invited anyone, but two from each gens. After indeed all had come, then the chief began serving them. After he had served them, he said, "It is done", to those celebrating the gens festival. "Very well", he was told.

Then the young man began to make a speech: "Now, so be it, we have offered this separately, so be it, to the Green Buffalo, so be it. It is life, so be it, that we mainly desire from him. He should wish this for us because of our tobacco, so be it. Pray, so be it, wish old age, so be it, for us because of our cooked food. That, so be it, is what we implore him, so be it. We do not desire, so be it, anything which is frightful. Indeed we ask him only what is good. That is why his fellow, so be it, chief, so be it, sits down at his feast, so be it. That is why you should eat, so be it. Eat, so be it", he said to them.

Those who were eating indeed ate slowly. They put away slowly the bones which were left over. After they had eaten the chief himself went to gather the bones. Then the ceremonial attendant put them away carefully. He placed them out of the path. And after the ceremonial attendant had returned, he then began to serve the pumpkins. There were four bowls. And one member of each gens was told to participate. They indeed went out and invited others. Each one indeed invited many. Then, it is said, they told when there was a sufficient number. "We are now of a sufficient number," the ceremonial attendant said to those celebrating the gens festival. Then the leading ceremonial attendant said to the leader of those giving the gens festival, "They have now all come."

Then the one blessed said, "So be it, from the buffaloes, so be it, whom we worship, so be it, life is what we desire, so be it. We, so be it, have talked of ourselves, so be it. So be it, we have asked them, so be it, that the manitous, so be it, may take us on to old age, so be it. He, the Spirit of Fire, so be it, has no doubt begun, so be it, long ago, so be it, to tell, so be it, our grandfather, so be it, about this. Again, so be it, we also extend our hands, so be it, to the buffaloes, so be it, who are here, so be it, on this earth, so be it, with our tobacco, so be it, and also, so be it, this, so be it, our cooked food, this pumpkin soup. They themselves, so be it, stated, so be it, that they would think highly of, so be it, pumpkins. They, so be it, should bless you accordingly, so be it, who have invited each other. They, so be it, have already said this, so be it, with respect to those, so be it, who shall eat these, so be it, carefully. They must, so be it, wish, so be it, old age for us, so be it, who eat carefully, so be it. Therefore, so be it, you must eat, so be it, you women, so be it, and you men, so be it. Eat!"

They ate. And after they had eaten he said to them, "Now sit, so be it, here where you have been seated, so be it, you women, so be it, and you men, so be it. There is much of this 'so be it' when the buffalo speech is given", he said to them. "You should carefully catch on, so be it, to the times when it is used. Now we had better start in singing", he said to them. "These are the same songs which we are to continue to use. There are not many of them, youths. This indeed is how we shall sing", he said to them:

When I arise here; etc.[10]
The buffaloes here tell me, "I fear you", yes; etc.[11]
This is why I have spoken, so I may be quoted; etc.[12]
The buffaloes here call me "the Green Buffalo"; etc.[13]

They danced.

I make it dance for you, I make it dance for you; etc.[14]
They, my fellow buffaloes, refer to me; etc.[15]
Father, I speak to you from afar; etc.[16]
He is instructed, he is instructed; etc.[17]

"We have now made them dance twice. There are yet two more times to make them dance. They will now eat some more food. They shall invite each other. They must indeed place some more food in the kettles in place of the food that has been eaten. The men will now indeed cook in a hurry", said the twin.

Then he spoke: "You who are a ceremonial attendant may eat from anywhere you desire. Indeed you ceremonial attendants must first have your bellies filled. After your bellies are filled, you will

---

[10] See pp. 41, 42. There are slight variations.

[11] See p. 42 with slight variations. The most important of these is a new half line, "They say of me, 'he is one-horned.' "

[12] See p. 42. The repetition in the present case is four times.

[13] See p. 42. Some slight variations may be due to errors in the syllabic script. A true variation, however, is the insertion of the line "The buffaloes here call me 'the Green Buffalo' " between the last two lines of the citations given.

[14] See p. 43. The variations which occur may be due to tremendous repetition of similar syllables; but in the present case the songs winds up A no se ni na "My father, I", which also may be due to faulty writing.

[15] See p. 43. Besides some possible graphic variations, in the present case wi na occurs everywhere for ni na, and an extra unfinished line Wi nwa wa A ne te ko ke ni tti (They, my fellow [buffaloes] refer to me) occurs at the end.

[16] See pp. 43, 44. The only variation of importance is that an extra line becomes the final one: Ke we to we e ne "I speak to you from afar"; while the final line that occurred the first time is omitted. In the sixth and seventh lines the present songs end in ne and have No se for No, respectively.

[17] See p. 44. The present song has seven lines as compared with six given previously. It has nothing corresponding to the line Na na i me ga na A na i me ga wi; on the other hand it has the refrain Na na i me ga na na i me ga four times before the line ending with wi na as compared with three times; and the final line given previously is repeated twice.

begin to be busy", he said to the ceremonial attendants. "You are then to serve the food to the women and children. You will feed them justly", he said to the ceremonial attendants.

The attendants then stopped to eat. And after they had eaten they started to serve the food. Indeed they went about it slowly. They started to serve the food beginning at the east, and they did so slowly. Moreover, one was outside inviting. A ceremonial attendant was inviting. There were indeed many to eat. After the attendants had served the food to those sitting inside they then began to serve food to those that had been invited. Later on they had indeed served all the food. "That is all", the ceremonial attendants said to the twin. "Very well", said the one who was giving the gens festival. He then began a speech.

"Well then, women and men, we have, so be it, first, so be it, scattered, so be it, our tobacco, so be it, to the Spirit of Fire, so be it, that he may tell for us in the right way, so be it, what, so be it, we ask, so be it, from the manitous, so be it. We ask, so be it, from them good health for our entire town, so be it. That, so be it, is what we ask, so be it, then to wish because of this, so be it, our cooked food. Again, should disease stand around, may our dwelling remain as manitous. That is, so be it, what we ask from those who are now seated, so be it, about, so be it, conspicuously, our grandfathers, so be it. They must think alike of our lives. That, so be it, is what we say to them, so be it. That verily, so be it, is why you are to eat, so be it, women and men. Eat!" he said to them.

The people now ate. They indeed consumed much food. Still, the ceremonial attendants put more food into the kettles. Then the young man said to those who were celebrating the gens festival with him, "Now we must sit quietly for a while." They sat still. "This sacred pack does not belong to me alone. We alike own it, even indeed a little baby. It owns it in just the same way that we own it. Still, I have been instructed with regard to it; but nevertheless I do not myself own the sacred pack. What it thinks of you it thinks of me. It does not love me alone. It loves you also just as much. How could it be that I should think that I claim the manitou's desire? It will not claim me alone. It has been placed here by the manitou so that we may worship it earnestly. Our grandfathers think the same of us. That one yonder is our greatest grandfather. At the time when he ruled our lives to be too short, he called together those who are called manitous. He told them what they must think of us. 'You must always love and bless the people.' That, it is said, is what he said to them. Still, those who are blessed by those told this, are taken up there. They are taken where the Great Manitou dwells. And when one is not taken up, the Great Manitou is summoned. He indeed looks at the one who has been blessed. Indeed the Great Manitou is simply of such a nature as to be shown the people. He will not refuse. Indeed he too must talk to one. Yet he is not to tell anyone that which is frightful. He must wish for the people that which is right. That is how he is. It is against his rules for the Great Manitou to wish the people that which is frightful. His wish for them is alone peacefulness. These others, however, might wish that. For it seems as if they have been made to wish for you whatever you may desire. 'You will continue to wish for them', they were told. It is impossible for the Great Manitou to say, 'You must not wish this for them.' That is why our grandfathers here continue to wish for us this, namely, 'I wish you to be a warrior.' The manitou has simply granted us that we make each other wail, back and forth. That is how he has arranged it for us. Even indeed some other little beings will do that to each other. They kill each other alternately. Indeed it has been fixed so for even the different kinds of little birds. One kind flies about at night. One kind flies about during the day. The one who flies about has enemies in accordance (with his time to fly). And we speak all sorts of different languages. That is how we have our enemies. That is why I say we take turns in making each other weep. No one alone will always make his fellow people weep. Indeed we are considered alike by the manitou who thinks over us. Yet our fasting is of different kinds. Our fasting does not think of us alike. Indeed our way is very hard. Again, whenever our womenfolk stay outside (i. e., are menstruating), they must stay outside. We must never eat with one who is staying outside (i. e., menstruating). That is what is expected of us. That is against the rules of these sacred packs. And a woman who is staying outside (i. e., menstruating) would be ruined by these sacred packs should she go inside where they are hanging. It is not only here where our sacred single pack hangs, but also where any sacred packs hang. That is how the manitou has preserved us.

"And also this. She must not look on during a gens festival such as we are holding. It is not that way. Indeed the same is so with every other gens festival. The one celebrating the gens festival should not allow them to look on. That is a thing that will be against our rules so long as there is an earth. Indeed it is said that soon we shall get so that we shall not care anything about this. When we cease to care anything about this, something will happen. It will be so if no one gives any gens festivals. It will not be so if one goes on and gives gens festivals. It will be after he ceases to think about it. Then the manitou will be ruled by it in turn. The manitou will call to this. If at that time the manitou has already called to it, then the things here will cease to grow. We then cannot eat anything. Indeed even this one who flies with wings will be gone. Indeed the little game will be gone. And the rivers will go down, indeed gradually. Now, what is there for us to eat? That which has made us to cease to think about our sacred packs will be around in abundance. It will then lie around everywhere.

"Still, we cannot indeed do anything about that at all. That will happen to those who will come far off from now. As it is now, it seems indeed as if we have just come to a hill for the first time. And we shall try to carry our sacred pack over it. I am now taking care of it. If I die then we shall carry it farther. Indeed finally we shall bring it up to the top of the hill, so it seems. As soon as we have taken it down a little way, there is where one dwells who cares nothing about it. From there, it seems, it will be rolled down the hill. It seems that after rolling down to the base, it will unwrap. That is the time when we shall fall here and there from hunger. And we cannot eat anything else", he said to them. "That is why I coax you to think about what I have told you. If some of our friends who sit yonder know anything about a sacred pack they would tell this same thing. Indeed they would not tell you anything different. They would say the same thing. Indeed I am telling you the plain truth", he said to his associates. "So I have once told you a tale."

Those who were invited were now through eating. "Now then, you may go to the places from where you were invited, for a while, women and men", he said to them.

The ceremonial attendants had now boiled food again. They had now cooked everything. Indeed they now were finally well filled. Then, it is said, he said to them: "These songs indeed are the ones we shall always use. These are those we shall use at first. Later on there will be many of them. These will not be the only songs we shall continue to use. Indeed these songs will increase just as long and as many times as we are victors on the warpath. It is not that we shall use all of them here at once. If the Buffaloes who are under the earth so desire we shall do that. Indeed he who goes out as the leader of a war party is he who will know what songs are to be added", he said to them. "I alone will not name them. He who heads a victorious war party is he who will be made to know by the manitou. That is how it is. I tell it to you in advance so that you will know what we are to do, and that you know what a difficult time we shall have in obtaining these songs. The songs of our friends are like this here and there. But ours are very difficult. If you desire to use them in a hurry you must fast. Indeed you will know the songs which we are to own at that time. Well, I am enjoying talking

too much; we had better start to sing", he said to the fellow
members of his gens. "Very well", they replied. They started
to sing. They again used the same songs which they had used.

When I arise here; etc.[18]
They tell me, "I fear you";
They fear me, yes;
They fear me; etc.[19]
This is why I have spoken, so I may be quoted; etc.[20]
The buffaloes here call me "the Green Buffalo";
The buffaloes here call me "the Green Buffalo"; etc.[21]

They had now sung. Then he said to them, "We are to be seated
for a while", he said to them. "This is why we are to be seated a
while: Our offerings have just been put in the kettles a short time ago.
That is why I have said, 'Let us be seated for a while' ", he said to
them. Then he said to them, "Well, our leaders, eventually we are
to dance."

I make it dance for you, I make it dance for you; etc.[22]
They, my fellow buffaloes, refer to me; etc.[23]
He is instructed, he is instructed; etc.[24]

"You are now to eat", the dancers were told. "Now, ceremonial
attendants, they are all to eat. You must all withdraw the kettles
from over the fire", the ceremonial attendants were told. "Since
you are ceremonial attendants you may indeed see whether you want
to eat or not", the ceremonial attendants were told. "You indeed
must serve them slowly. Do not be in a hurry while serving food to
those who sit about. Indeed be slow. Again, those who are to
issue invitations are to be two in number. The Ō'ckA'cA (Tō'kānA)
may go toward the east, and the Kī'ckō'A toward the west. That
is what they are to do. One of them must be a member of the War
Chiefs gens and one of them must be a member of the Bear gens.
There will be exactly two of them. They will not walk as if they were
trying to beat each other. They indeed are to walk around slowly
when they walk to give invitations. The only persons whom they
are not to invite are those who are disabled. The food may be carried
to those who are thus disabled. They may eat yonder. They may
indeed say to the children, 'I invite you.' Indeed they must continue

---

[18] See pp. 41, 42, 46. There are variations, mostly not serious.

[19] See pp. 42, 46. There are variations, the most important of which is the absence of anything corre-
ponding to "The buffaloes here."

[20] See pp. 42, 46. There are no variants from p. 42.

[21] See pp. 42, 46. There are but minor variations from the first reference which is used as a standard here,
and similarly elsewhere. The most important variants are in the repetition of the line A yo ko   ne no so ke
twice instead of once, the first time it occurs; and its single occurrence terminally instead of twice.

[22] See pp. 43, 46. There is nothing corresponding to lines 4 and 5 of the song on p. 43; and the terminal
portion is lacking.

[23] See pp. 43, 46. The first four lines do not differ from the song given on p. 43, save that terminal wi na
occurs for ni na in the third line. There is nothing corresponding to line 5. The last line is repeated twice.

[24] See pp. 44, 46. The present song differs from the one on p. 46 in that it has no line ending with wi na;
instead Na na i me ga   na A na i me ga occurs.

to say that to them. That is what the manitous say to each other.
Just for fun they say to each other, 'I invite you.' For that reason
they may go about saying that to them. Indeed they must even
say to babies in their cradles, 'I invite you.' They must say that to
them and mention their names. They are indeed to walk around
slowly. Wherever they happen to meet each other there is from
where they are to return. And those of you who are here may then
begin serving the food to those who have been invited. That is what
you must do. You are not to serve them in a hurry. You must
serve those who are to eat slowly. Indeed you may eat after they
have all come. You must not proceed to inform us. Every one
of you must indeed think about life. You must think about it in
your hearts. 'I wish I could live to that time.' That is what we are
to think. 'I wish that I may reach the full length of my life.' That
is what we are to think in our hearts. Again 'I wish that disease
may not strike me.' That is what we must also think in our hearts."

The one celebrating the gens festival said the same things to all.
And, it is said, those invited began to come in. As the people came in
they were served food. Then there was no more room inside the
dwelling and they had to sit outside. And, it is said, after the people
had started to sit outside, the leading ceremonial attendants went
outside to serve the food. The people who had been invited came
continuously. There was humming everywhere as the people talked
to each other.

Indeed some time later they saw the inviters coming as a pair.
Then the one celebrating the gens festival said, "Now you no doubt
are keeping track of what we are doing. You must keep track very
carefully of what we are to do. These people are indeed to eat all at
once. We shall do this so the food may be eaten all at once. Our
offerings must not be left over. That is not our way. The manitou
has desired us to do it this way. It seems as if this worship were
spilled. Then the lives we were to get were thrown away. That life
which is thrown away is not somebody else's but our own. Indeed
it seems that should someone have a weak life, then his life would end
indeed quickly. Indeed his life would go backward. That is what
would happen to him. Again, our children would be those who would
continue to die. It seems as if a child's life is weak. Because it is a
child is why it barely lives. That is why it would continue to die.
It is the same with regard to the life of the aged. Indeed that is
precisely my reason in forbidding our offerings to be left over. That
is why I tell you that. When you hold your gens festivals have the
right amount of offerings. Do not be dissatisfied with the amount of
your offerings in the gens festivals. As it is now, it is very likely that
we have the right amount for this gens festival. If they could barely
consume it, then we should offer less in our next gens festival. Then

indeed we shall know the amount we are to offer in our worship of the manitou. The manitou himself does not desire that we offer him much food in our worship. Indeed it makes no difference if the offering is little when we worship him. He would consider it much. It is then made into any amount that is desired. If indeed the manitou desires that there be much of it, he can make much from it. When he is offered much of it, it is considered the same. That is why you should continue to tell one another. Indeed you should continue to tell each other. Indeed the manitou is truly a manitou. We should do whatever he has wished. If he blesses us he will never forget us. Indeed we shall be remembered just as there is a people. We see this earth and this sky as reminders. We do not know when they are to go to ruin. Very likely later on it will be desired that they change. Even in the same way you who are still remembered will see each other. And you will not see each other in few numbers. Still, it is very hard indeed to have the manitou pity you and to have him think about you. Indeed that is what you should continue to tell each other. Why should you lie to each other about this? It is all right", he said to them. "That is what I have to say to you", he said to them.

Then he was informed, "We have now served all the food to all. Indeed the food was exactly enough. There was not too little, and there was none left over."

Then, it is said, he said to them, "Now when I begin to give my speech this time, you must all think alike in your hearts about our offerings. Every one of you has been made to sit down to this offering by the ceremonial attendants. You are not to talk to each other for a while. Do just whatever I have told you, that is, think alike in your hearts", he said to them. "This is what you must think, 'I wish I could reach old age.' You must think that as you sit down with this offering. That indeed is the way. And also this. 'I wish I could become a man and could easily deal with my enemy.' That is what you must think of. 'Think of me in the same way as you think of the one whom you have blessed.' That also is what you must think. That is what I have to tell you. If you think in your hearts, 'Who is there who will know what we think in our hearts?' (be it known that) there is a manitou called 'He Who Lies With His Face Bulging In The Smoke-Hole.' He is the one who will know what you think in your hearts. That one was told to come down here and live with the people. He was instructed to come here so that he might know what we think in our hearts about our lives. Indeed he is the one who is to tell all our hearts' desires. That is what he has been told. He will not tell falsely what we think about our lives. He will tell all of the manitous who have blessed me. There will be none of them who do not know about us", he said to the people. "So indeed think that way", he said to them, "women and men." "All right" they replied.

"When, so be it, I made, so be it, the manitou, so be it, take compassion, so be it, upon me he did not, so be it, wish, so be it, me that which is evil, so be it. He wished me, so be it, that, so be it, which was good, so be it. This is, so be it, the first time, so be it, we will worship him, so be it. He has stated, so be it, that I would tell the truth, so be it, in here, so be it. So, if, so be it, if all of you, so be it, who are tasting, so be it, my offerings, so be it, for the first time, so be it, if you indeed think, so be it, alike, so be it, then, so be it, his life will be, so be it, exactly, so be it, the way he desires, so be it. Again, so be it, we shall chew the war enemies soft, so be it, of the one whose relatives, so be it, have been wronged, so be it. This is what we shall wish for such a one, so be it, that in return, so be it, he, so be it, will make them sad, so be it. That, so be it, is what the manitous, so be it, who sit, so be it, under this earth, so be it, told me, so be it, when, so be it, they blessed me, so be it. We speak first, so be it, to the manitou buffalo, so be it, who sits facing us, so be it, yonder in the east, so be it. He must wish life for us, so be it, in return, so be it, for our cooked food, so be it. And we have also, so be it, raised up our hands collectively, so be it, with tobacco. 'Wish that, so be it, for us because of our tobacco, so be it.' That, so be it, is what we say to him, so be it. And again, so be it, wish that some of them, so be it, be men (i. e., warriors), so be it. That, so be it, is what we say to him, so be it. Again, may our entire town, so be it, never, so be it, be entered by this disease, so be it. That, so be it, is what we say to him, so be it. Think, so be it, and wish life, so be it, only, so be it, for our town, so be it. That, so be it, is what we ask, so be it, from the buffalo, so be it, who sits, so be it, facing us from the east, so be it. He himself, so be it, has promised, so be it, what we would think about us, so be it, so that he thereby might derive his smoke from here, so be it.

"And also, so be it, the one who spoke to me the second time, so be it, the Sunny Buffalo, so be it, who sits, so be it, in the south, so be it, has also, so be it, spoken that way, so be it. 'When you (sing.) first worship, so be it, me I will think of every one of you, so be it, in your town, so be it.' That is the way they spoke, so be it, when they first, so be it, blessed me, so be it. He also, so be it, has told, so be it, what he would wish for us, so be it. 'I will wish life, so be it, for every one of them, so be it, who has been affected, so be it, by your worship, so be it.' That, so be it, is what he also, so be it, has told me, so be it. 'And again, if he desires, so be it, (the enemy) from without, so be it, who has made him weep, so be it, I will, so be it, chew, so be it, him soft for him, so be it.' That is, so be it, what, so be it, the Sunny Buffalo, so be it, has said, so be it. That, so be it, is what we ask, so be it, from him. Also, so be it, that he think, so be it, quietly of our town, so be it. That is, so be it, what he, so be it, has said, so be it. And if disease, so be it, should pass by here, so be it, may it not enter, so be it, here. That is, so be it, what we ask, so be it, the Sunny Buffalo, so be it, to wish for us, so be it.

"And, so be it, the buffalo, so be it, who sits facing us, so be it, from the west, so be it, has also told me that, so be it. I ask, so be it, from him, so be it, that which he has told me, so be it. When he said, 'When you first, so be it, worship me, so be it, and someone is first, so be it, made to realize, so be it, this by your worship, so be it, he will indeed be so loaded (?), so be it, as to reach old age', so be it. That is, so be it, what we ask from him, so be it, that which he has already said, so be it. 'And if he desires his war enemies, so be it, in any way, so be it, indeed, so be it, I shall wish that for him, so be it, or whatever, so be it, he desires, so be it. If he only, so be it, desires, so be it, old age, so be it, indeed, so be it, I shall wish for him, so be it, that which he has asked.' Indeed, so be it, that is how, so be it, he spoke, so be it, when he spoke to me, so be it. 'And, so be it, when this diesease stands around your town, so be it, your dwellings will stand as manitous. It cannot, so be it, enter your dwelling, so be it. I shall only, so be it, quietly, so be it, wish it away for you.' That is, so be it, what the buffalo, so be it, told me, so be it, when he spoke to me, so be it. He must wish us that, so be it. He must wish us that, so be it, because of our tobacco, so be it, as we raise our hands upward, so be it, with it, so be it. And they must also think the same, so be it, because of our cooked food, so be it. They, so be it, have already said, so be it, that themselves, so be it. That is the reason, so be it, why I have confidently reminded them thereof, so be it.

"Then again, so be it, the Wintry Buffalo, so be it, who sits facing us from the north, so be it, has also told me the same, so be it. 'When you first, so be it, worship me, so be it, why I shall indeed, so be it, bless, so be it, every one, so be it, of your, so be it, fellow people, so be it, who is first affected by your worship.' What we have now told them, so be it, is what, so be it, they must wish us, so be it. And if some one's relatives have been slain, the slayer will be chewed soft in return. That, so be it, is what, so be it, we desire, so be it, the Wintry Buffalo, so be it, to wish for us, so be it. 'And, so be it, if anyone wants, so be it, old age, so be it, only, indeed I shall wish him that, so be it.' That is what the manitous, so be it, who blessed me said. And, so be it, this, so be it, Spirit of Fire, so be it, must so remind them, so be it. He, so be it, has been named, so be it, as the one upon whom, so be it, we are to depend, so be it, our grandfather, so be it.

"That is what our grandfathers also, so be it, must think of us. We do not, so be it, only ask them, so be it, what they must think

about us alone, so be it. Indeed they must think that, so be it, of
every one of us, so be it, children, so be it, as well as, so be it, women,
so be it, and men, so be it. Whatever we desire them to wish for us
is now granted us. We have now implored the manitous what to
think of us. After all, so be it, they will be reminded of it as they
smoke our tobacco. Indeed, so be it, that is what we say to them.
They may, so be it, thus, so be it, speak to each other, so be it. We
are then to do, so be it, whatever we have desired for ourselves. That
is all. Oh, so be it, they will not, so be it, merely say this, so be it.
They are not too small, so be it, to think, so be it. We shall now, so
be it, all alike request the same from this Spirit of Fire, so be it. He
has, so be it, probably begun long ago, so be it, to tell, so be it, his
fellow manitous, so be it. And, so be it, the one called 'He Who
Knows Inner Thoughts', so be it, will begin to tell, so be it, what we
think, so be it, about our lives, so be it, so be it. Again, those who
desire, so be it, to become warriors, so be it, will be granted, so be it,
their desires, so be it, by the manitous, so be it, whom we worship,
so be it. The manitous, so be it, must think that way of every one
of us, so be it. They, so be it, are those who own those desires. They,
so be it, must think that, so be it, of us. They themselves, so be it,
our grandfathers, so be it, have already told me, so be it. Verily
now, so be it, you women, so be it, and you men, so be it, ought to
begin, so be it, eating, so be it. Eat!" he said to them.

The people ate slowly. There surely were many. They ate for
some time. Indeed their bellies were exactly well filled. No one
was too full. Indeed the eaters had their bellies filled each alike.
It is said that there was much food which they had eaten. Still
they had indeed consumed it all.

Then the one celebrating the gens festival said to his fellow members while the eating took place: "I have now just told you about
this. We shall now each alike have strong lives. I have told these
people what they must think in their hearts about their lives. Some
of them have desired what I have told them. And some did not think
about that at all. Still, they will be thought of in the manner the
manitou thinks of us. They will not be thought of in the way they
desired. It is only he who has thought in the way I have indicated
who will be thought of in whatever way he desired. He who has
desired to be thought of in another way will not be thought of at all.
The manitou has told what we must desire from him. He who
desires this is he who will be thought of by him. That is the only
way I know how to be blessed by him. If one has the privilege of
desiring to be thought of in another way, he will not be thought of.
Only he who thinks about his life in exactly the way I have said, is
he who is known by the manitou, and by those leading beings whom
I have mentioned in a circle (i. e., in east, south, west, and north).

They indeed are the leading ones who have been made to watch over our desires. They have mentioned that they would all join in thinking about us at this time. This day we have thought of them indeed for the first time. They told me to tell everyone what to think. That is indeed why I have told everyone. Well, at this time we shall begin singing. Yet we shall stop to tell them and thereby remind them. It is a rule that everyone must dance. That is what we must stop to tell them", he said to them. He spoke to them himself.

"Well, this time you must all dance for us", he said to them. "After we sing we are to sing dancing songs", he said to them. "You must then think about what I have told you. Indeed you must do so", he said to them. The people everywhere replied favorably. They were indeed willing to dance. "Well, our leading ceremonial attendant, we shall want your services for a while right here", he said to him. Then he said to the attendant, "These are not to return home after eating." Then he informed those who were seated about outside. "It is said that you are not to return home", the ceremonial attendants said to them. They indeed remained seated. Then at last they began singing.

When I arise here; etc.[25]
They tell me, "I fear you"; etc.[26]
This is why I have spoken, so I may be quoted; etc.[27]
The buffaloes here call me "the Green Buffalo"; etc.[28]

"At last we are going to make you dance, our friends. You will make us willing if every one of you dance", he said to them.

I make it dance for you, I make it dance for you; etc.[29]
They, my fellow buffaloes, refer to me; etc.[30]
Father, I speak to you from afar; etc.[31]
He is instructed, he is instructed; etc.[32]
If the chieftainess here uses (?);
If she uses this warning here;
[Repeat four times.]

[Yo we ki ma ge wi ta gi se A yo te;
Yo ke na na ma A mo ne A yo te;]
[Repeat four times.]

---

[25] See pp. 41, 42, 46, 50. The following are the most important variations from the song on pp. 41, 42: The fifth line is repeated three times; then follow A yo gi se as the last line.

[26] See pp. 42, 46, 50. The song corresponds for all purposes to that given on p. 50.

[27] See pp. 42, 46, 50. There are no variations from the song on p. 42.

[28] See pp. 42, 46, 50. The following are the deviations from the song on p. 42: The third line is repeated twice; ski la ki ne no swa occurs in place of ski la ki ne no so; the last line is line 6. It is closer then to the song on p. 50.

[29] See pp. 43, 46, 50. The song varies considerably from that given on p. 43. It agrees with that on p. 46 as far as the terminal line is concerned. Otherwise it is close to the song on p. 50.

[30] See pp. 43, 46, 50. The present song consists of the first line of the song on p. 43 repeated four times.

[31] See pp. 43, 44, 46. The song agrees substantially with the one given on p. 46.

[32] See pp. 44, 46, 50. There are seven lines, all being the same as the first line of the song on p. 44. It therefore approximates the song on p. 50.

"We have now made you dance", he said to them. "And when dancing songs are used for the third time, these dancing songs are indeed used. That is the way it is. You should keep track of how they all are. The third time only three dancing songs are used", he said to them.

There were indeed many people. He was yet seated. "Now, my friends, I have told you some time ago that you should think of yourselves, what you should desire to be thought of by the manitous who blessed me. Indeed you did not all alike believe me. Some did not think in their hearts what I said for them to think. Indeed some thought about something totally different. Indeed they did not desire what I told them to desire. They have thus disbelieved me. And if we were to see the manitou suddenly, we could not indeed tell him our desires the same way. This, it seems, would happen to us. Our desires would be strung all over. We should not do what indeed would please the manitou. It seems that we shall only ask that which will make our lives good. That is what we alike say to the manitou. He would not refuse us. And if we desire from him different things he would not know whom to believe. Very likely the manitou would be discouraged if we asked too many things from him. Very likely someone would ask something which he hates. He indeed would not be told, 'I dislike that (to be your wish)', if he said to him, 'this is how you will bless me.' That is how it now looks. Some ask that all sorts of things may be granted them. Even some old men ask for women. And a woman asks the same thing. He does not like that very well. For somewhere there is seated one who bestows such blessings. That is what I have to stop to tell you.

"Now who is there who would think in his heart, 'Gracious!' when his worship has just been completed? Perhaps, so be it, we thus have pleased our grandfathers. They probably would not think in their hearts, 'It shall not be.' We no doubt have made our grandfathers' hearts glad because we have eaten this which is extended to them with our hands. We have, so be it, raised our hands up to those manitous. Indeed you have probably thereby pleased them. They will always be that way. That is what I wish these grandchildren of mine. That is what they should think of us. As for you, our grandfathers should think the same of you. And they think indeed the same of these ceremonial attendants. Indeed they should wish them to reach old age after carefully handling all of our offering. We all have indeed worshiped them. We alone did not worship them. Indeed we pleaded that they think of all of us alike. We were to have indeed desired the same. Yet we did not desire the same. Therefore you had better depart to where you live, women, and also you men."

Then the people walked off in different directions. When they came to where they came from, those who believed thought in their hearts, "Oh, this is what he has said."

It is said that they would know that as soon as they went to sleep. Truly some indeed obtained what they had asked.

Then that member of the Wolf gens indeed led a war party. He too thought in his heart, "I shall carry my sacred pack about. It may indeed be that there will be no one who will carry it for me", he said to them. " 'Very likely someone will carry it off', I thought", he said to them. Then he was informed by many who desired to become warriors. And he addressed them: "Now men, I do not want many, I only want men from four households. Indeed there must be just that number—four. Indeed our enemy will not harm us in any way. Indeed they will all alike be brought here. Indeed it seems as if this which I am to carry about will bring them. Let no one be afraid of those whom I have already eaten. They are those whom I have already eaten. What is there then that will make you fear them? Indeed let no one think of fearing them. Indeed I am now telling you assuredly what you will do to them. You must not stop to deal gently with them. That is why I have told you. There will be four households of them. Indeed there will be precisely so many. And indeed you must go about and beat our enemies' heads until they sound. Indeed even if they have something which hurts, it will be nothing. Indeed it will be ruined before they have a chance to use it on us. That is what will happen to them. That is why I tell you that you can go at them to your heart's desire. What is there then that will make you fear them?" he said to them.

"If you should turn and run, then indeed they would see just which of us they shoot at. That is what I have to say to you. Indeed should they even hold knives in their hands they will indeed drop them when they start to take after us. That is what I have to tell you. Indeed you must think earnestly of what I have told you. You must indeed do what I have told you. Still, it may be that we shall not return for a while, or we might come upon them easily. Indeed we might come to them later on. Where they will stay will not be in this direction. If you think in your hearts, 'We shall come upon them quickly', then indeed we will quickly come upon them. Indeed you may do as you desire", he said to them.

The one who carried about the scared pack with him was the ceremonial attendant who belonged to the War Chiefs gens. And he told his ceremonial attendant, "You must inform me what they have to say, ceremonial attendant." Then he listened while they counselled. Some thought they should search for them slowly. And some thought they should find them quickly. And those who thought they should find them quickly were believed. "Indeed we shall do

that. We shall indeed see them quickly", they said. "Very well",
they were told. They then told that ceremonial attendant so he
might tell about it. And he told the leader of the war party. "They
said that they would see them quickly", so he said to him. "Very
well", the other replied. "Then you must go hunting very early
tomorrow. If you kill an elk before sunrise, then indeed it will be so.
It will not be so if it is killed later. Indeed the one who kills the elk
will be the one to kill the enemy first. You will bring the elk in
quickly. Then you will butcher it. If you dress it carefully and
without trouble we will be masters of what we are to do. Indeed at
this time they may go hunting very early in every direction. Why,
they have wished us to see the foe quickly", he said to them.

Then that ceremonial attendant was told to go over and tell them
that at least. He indeed told them just what he had been told.
Those people, those belonging to the war party, were proud. And
the hunters went out early in the morning. After they had walked
a little way, a man killed an elk. He was proud. He already thought
in his heart that he would be the first to slay a foe. Some of them
envied the man. They brought the large elk in. "You must indeed
butcher it quickly", the men were told. And the ceremonial attendant was awakened after it had been butchered. "You alone must
roast and eat it", the ceremonial attendant was told. He started
to roast much of it. After he had cooked it, he started to untie that
sacred pack. "Indeed this is what I am going to worship", he was
told. After he sat down to his roasted meat, then the one whom he
served as a ceremonial attendant began to make a speech. This is
what he said:

"Now, so be it, we shall rely on the manitou, so be it, who sits, so
be it, yonder, so be it, in the east, so be it. He will, so be it, indeed
bring, so be it, the hearts of those whom I shall attack, so be it. You
will therefore eat this. Eat", he was told.

The ceremonial attendant ate heartily. After he had eaten alone
he was told: "Ceremonial attendant, cut it up in pieces." He cut it
up in pieces. Then he was told, "Ceremonial attendant, go around
and give it to our friends. I also will even eat. Indeed every one
of us may eat, for you have eaten the one I offered in my gens festival.
We shall now eat this one." That is what the young man said.
"You may indeed give everyone the same amount. Each gens shall
have the same amount. We shall eat that way", he said. Indeed
they then, every one of them, ate with the members of their respective
gentes. For example, the ceremonial attendant ate with the members
of the War Chiefs gens. They sat in no particular places. And after
they had eaten they were told, "Now indeed you will put out the
fire every place." And those whose business it was put the fire out

everywhere. Then they were told, "We shall listen very quietly." They listened to learn who was going on the warpath.

Suddenly they saw where there was light. There were four lights burning. "There it is, men", they were told. Then the ceremonial attendant was told to go and watch as a scout. "Very well", he replied. He departed. He came yonder to where the Sioux were staying. He counted how many men there were. And he also counted the number of women. He departed. He returned to the place from which he had departed. "Well, ceremonial attendant, what did you observe?" "I could not look at them closely, that is, I could not go inside their dwellings." He started to tell how many Sioux there were, and how many in each household. Then he was told, "That's it, ceremonial attendant. You please me. I thought in my heart as you walked away, 'I wish he would count.' Indeed you have done just what I desired you to do", he said to him. "You shall indeed kill one who has the nature of a manitou. I have indeed told you to do this so that I may always think in my heart, 'This ceremonial attendant is one who has a being who has the nature of a manitou' ", he said to his ceremonial attendant. The ceremonial attendant was proud.

Then they started to creep upon their foes. They lay down close to them. Just as soon as it was light enough to see they attacked them. They whooped at them and knocked them around until their heads sounded with each stroke. The scouts were all struck down. Then the war party went home. They were joyous on their way. Surely they had not been harmed by their foes. And they were cheered on their way. Indeed no one felt sad in his heart as they were returning. And when the men returned everywhere their relatives were proud. "That's it", the men were told. Indeed every one of them became warriors. Every one of those young men now loved the one whom they accompanied. Indeed they would always invite him whenever they ate. They always did that to the one by whom they had been made warriors.

And later on that man again departed. "Now, men, where I am going is dangerous. Very likely you will indeed shoot each other's flesh back and forth until it sounds", he said to them. Then indeed some returned. They were afraid. That was why they returned. Indeed there were many who had been made afraid by his talk. That was why they returned. Finally those who were not able to return came to the spot. "You now know how many of you there are. You may go and cheer the food which I have left over where I have been summoned to eat. There is not much of it now. There is but a single one whom I am going to attack. He who has gone home has simply gone home. There is one person whom I shall go to attack. It is one that is lost. So that he will not simply starve to death, it is said, is why I am to attack him. It indeed has been said that he is thought of evilly by a manitou. It is said that is the only thing that is considered best for him, so that he will not be worried any more by traveling. Indeed he would always think in his heart of where he came from. Indeed after he is gone, it is said, he will remain just in one place. That is considered best by the one who thinks of him. If he is killed he will not die naturally. It is said it would be shameful for him to starve to death. It is said he would lie in shame. Therefore I shall go and be fed. I hold him in my mouth. Indeed you are not to fear him. I have already dissolved him in my mouth", he said to those whom he accompanied. "This is the way he will come", he said to them. "He will have only a single weapon. He will indeed be satisfied with it. He indeed is one who has been starved. That is the one I am to attack. And indeed you will get him unmercifully", he said to those whom he had taken.

Those who accompanied him were few in number. He told them what they had to do. And they did exactly so. They waited to see where the foe would come into view. It is said that they really saw that man. Indeed when he came close they whooped. He indeed only looked at them. They all ran toward him. It is said that he threw away his bow and jumped down on his knees. He raised his hands upward. He then was not killed. He was taken. Indeed it is said that they fed him well. That, it is said, is what they did to him. And they took him along. And indeed during his stay he learned to talk Indian (i. e., Fox). After he could speak Indian well he began to relate what had happened to him during the time he was lost. He indeed never mentioned who his parents were. He was asked, "Have you any parents?" "No", he replied. "I was wretched when I was a child", he said. "My fellow Indians deserted me when I was sick", he replied. "Whenever you go on the warpath yonder I indeed will go with you. I am going to capture those who deserted me", he said to them.

And one man who desired to go on the warpath fasted. That Indian went with the one who took care of the sacred pack. And later a war party went yonder on the warpath. Indeed he accompanied them. The man who took care of him stayed at home. Indeed the (captive) now could speak Indian well. He also walked along anywhere when they went on the warpath. Later on they attacked. And he captured those who had deserted him. Later they recognized him. He cheered against them. Indeed he captured those who had treated him so very cruelly. He took along those whom he captured. Indeed he brought them to where he was staying. He gave his fellow Indians to the one with whom he was staying. "Indeed I went after them because they treated me very cruelly. I did not go after them for no reason: They deserted me when I was disabled. So you can do with them whatever you desire.

If you wish to club them to death right here you may club them to death", he said to him. And the other replied, "The ceremonial attendant is the one who should club these to death." The ceremonial attendant was summoned. "Well, ceremonial attendant, you are to club these to death. You must wait and bring them inside my dwelling. After you have brought them inside, then you will club them to death", the ceremonial attendant was told. Then, it is said, they were taken over there to him. The people were many. He took them inside. After they were taken inside he went to kill them. There was a soft sound. Later, a scalp came out; and then another. Indeed as many as there were, were all clubbed to death. Indeed all he did was to throw out the scalps. Whenever he threw them out the men would seize them from each other. And he became a warrior. And at last he said, "Where are the warriors?" "These are they", they said to him. "Well, they are to take these whom they have killed and throw them away", he said to them. They took them off.

Then the member of the Wolf gens spoke: "This ceremonial attendant of mine has been made a man (i. e., a brave) by the manitou. Indeed he will always do that to his fellow people. He will not wish to deal gently with them. He is not made to do that. Indeed he will not deal gently with any little thing. That is what he is to do. If he tells about the time he was spoken to, we would hear horrors." That is what the member of the Wolf gens said. And when he came yonder he jumped and lay down. They did not know what the matter was with him, so it is said. He had died. "It is too bad", the people said. This is the end.

NOTES

This is one thing in which they believe: A long time ago when children were losing their teeth they were told to exchange their teeth with those of garter snakes. The children went around the wickiups four times and threw the tooth to the east.

And another thing in which they strongly believed was to keep clean. Our forefathers bathed. They bathed every morning. They even bathed every morning throughout the winter.

There is another thing to which they are opposed today: It is not to have their fingernails grow out. This is one of the things they hate to see on a person.

And another thing: When girls menstruate for the first time they are placed quite a distance from the wickiups. They are supposed to be there for 20 days. When they first menstruate they are usually cut with a razor on their legs and made to bleed. And now they will not allow such girls to eat for 2 days.

And when they first have a child this is how they are treated: Two women hold the girl who is going to have the child by the arms.

And this is how they do. By doing this they will not have a hard time at the next childbirth.

And this is another thing they did: In the early spring they usually gathered and smoked themselves with white leaves. This is what they did before going on the warpath. They sat in a circle with only breechcloths on. And the womenfolk also came. And they wore a single garment. They also sat in a circle. They had all these regulations in the early days. They did this before hunting. That is why they feared nothing. And it is claimed that this was one of the ways they should have kept up. It was a long time ago when they used to keep these laws.

Another thing: When anyone treated a girl evilly—if he made her pregnant, he was killed. This was their law. So that did not happen. They used to have a very strict law.

Another thing: It was against their law to marry within their own gens, but now they haven't this rule. They use the white man's law. It was fine when the Indians' law was used. It was hard. If anyone was caught doing wrong he was killed. This was the law in the early days. Our old men claim it was the best law.

This is how these religions are: There was once a man who fasted 4 days. He was blessed by a manitou; and he was given this "Menstruating Society" [Myānōtäwʌ'ckwä'iweni]. This is what happened to him. While he slept he was addressed by someone, and shown this: He looked at it. As he looked at it it was bloody. He took good notice of it. It was a woman. She was bloody all over. And this blood was dried and put into little bundles. After it was thoroughly dried these were placed in little packs. And after he was told this he woke up and went home. He was told that he would be instructed again. He was told to return 2 days later. So he returned and was told what to do. After he returned the manitou who conferred the blessing made those packs. And a fire was built. After a fire had been built a bowl was made out of earth. And after this was done some of the blood was placed there. And after the manitou had done this he went around in a circle. As the manitou went around the fire he shook his arms. After he had gone around four times the man himself was asked to do so. After he had done so the manitou began showing him songs. He raised his hands upward.

I am, I am a manitou;
I am, I am a manitou.

And he raised one hand upward and uttered mystic cries. And this is the second song:

I am the one the manitou saw;
I am the only one.

There are very many manitous who have blessed the people. Some of those blessings are true and some are weak. And this is what they say: "My grandfather, now today I have given you tobacco, praying for life." They raise up one of their hands when they pray. While they do this the ceremonial attendant is supposed to get the food out of the kettle. That is what members of the Menstruating Society do. After the food is placed in wooden bowls they call upon warriors, only warriors. And they wore no clothing except breechcloths. This was the way in the early days. They circled around the fireplace four times when they first entered. This was the rule in the early days. They ate the brains of dogs the first time there was eating.

And about the Thunder gens: This is one thing which is against their religion. It is this: They should not draw anything on the west side of a tree. And they should not pour water on themselves when naked. This is a strict rule. They still have that law.

And about the Fish gens: They also have ways that members must not transgress. One is, they must not build a dam. This is against their ways. They must not do so in any stream.

And the Bear gens are restricted by regulations which must not be violated. They must not sit in trees. This means any tree that grows. This rule is held at the present time.

And Those Named After the Buffalo dare not skin any cloven-hoofed animal. And they teach each other not to look at these animals at the time they die. This is strictly adhered to at the present time.

And about the Wolf gens: Members must not bury anyone belonging to their gens. It is against their religion. They dare not strike dogs of any kind. This is a strict rule for them.

And about the Morning Birds (Wâpᴀnowᴀgi): They must not kill any kind of flying creatures. And they also teach their children not to harm birds; nor to disturb the eggs nor the nests. This is a strict rule for the Morning Birds.

And the Dirty Little Ani should not dig in the ground. This is still a strict rule.

And the members of the Eagle gens should not place a feather on their heads. They still teach this to each other.

And the War Chiefs (error for Kindly Chiefs) should not say anything against a human being. This is still enforced.

And the members of the Beaver gens should not wade across rivers. There are only a few of them at the present time. But at the present time it is a strict rule.

And the White Wolves should not cry out at the top of their voices. This is against their religion even at the present time.

There was a gens which exists no more. The members dared not own anything. They could not have pets. They could not own even a dog. That is how that gens was.

And another thing about those belonging to the White Buffalo Society: Nothing is against their religion. They are not as particular as others. In case a death occurs in all the gentes there is only one particular speech which they have. Yet they have their own songs. Each gens has its own songs. Those are wailing songs. These are the songs they use, merely wailing songs.

Another thing that is different in each gens: It is the painting. They all paint differently. That is how it is. And their clothes differ according to gentes. And they have different things to cook at their festivals. Some of them only use pumpkins and beans when anyone dies. And this is what they use.

A corpse is always placed at the west end of dwellings. People should be out digging graves early in the morning, as early as they can. And this is their way. Different gentes have this regulation. They also send tobacco. And they usually place tobacco on the fingers of the corpse. They also send food, they say. And when they have an adoption feast after the adopted has been clad whenever he leaves the place, the adopters usually follow him for a short distance. This means they are sorry. Another thing they do is to kill a dog. And the dogs are placed at the west end of the grave. And it is still done at the present time. These are the groups that are supposed to bury each other: The Bear gens and the Wolf gens bury each other; [1] the Thunder gens and Dirty Little Ani; the Eagle gens and the Beaver gens; the War Chiefs and Those Named After the Buffalo; the Menstruating Society and the Fish gens.

In the early days people used to fast. And this is how they received their religion. And they were not afraid to fast.

And when the people are "unreleased" widows and widowers this is their rule: They must not touch horses or ponies. And another thing, widows and widowers must not go by gardens, nor fields. If they do they will dry them up. And this is a strict rule. Another thing: They dare not touch any human being, nor a child. And they are told not to swim in rivers. It is said that rivers belong to the manitou. That is the reason they do not allow widows or widowers who are unreleased to get into the water. And that is what has happened. When they have to cross rivers they usually wrap themselves in deerskin. That is the only way they can cross. And they still believe this at the present time.

And these White Wolves: Whenever they die in the summer the corpses are placed without covering at night.

Another thing they did formerly: In order to keep corpses from being spoiled they used to cut the veins of arms and suck out the blood. They used to use small deer horns or buffalo horns. They claim by doing this the body will not smell so badly. And when a

---

[1] The informant on direct interrogation says years ago White Buckskin and some other warriors made some changes. These became mixed, and subsequently old men tried to straighten out the changes. The informant claims the Wolf gens-War Chiefs arrangement is modern. Among the literary remains of the late Dr. William Jones I find a statement by PA'citōnĭgwA, the last recognized Fox chief, which supports Thunder and Wolf reciprocity.

woman died they sucked the blood at the top of the calves of her legs, just under the knees.

And when young men became warriors they made them drink deer blood. But they do not do this today. This formerly was a strict rule. Today we have no warriors.

And when the White Wolves celebrate their festival they have four dogs. This is late in summer. And they tie them against a tree. It must be an oak tree. One is on the east side, another the south, another the west, another the north. When the feast is over they tie the dogs against the tree. This is the business of the ceremonial attendants. The leading ceremonial attendant is the one who looks after this, and he only.

Another thing that is still going on: They place the bones west of where the ceremonies are taking place. They pile them against a tree. This is still their strict belief. They still do so.

And this is something which they have dropped. It is a rule which they used to observe: It is to have women warriors place the kettles on the fires, the very first kettle. They were supposed to do so. But they do not do so today as there are no women warriors. Formerly there were women warriors. And this is how there came to be women warriors: When the foes were killed their bodies were brought over and the women were made to strike them. These women are those whom they called "warrior women." They used to take care of the first kettle. And they used to drum. That is what they did in the early days. This is one of the things which they dropped long ago.

And in the spring when the strawberries are ripe this is another thing they do: Whenever they first see a strawberry they pick it and go in the woods to get a mayapple leaf. And they place the leaf on the ground and place the strawberry and tobacco on top of it. This is another way of making a sacrifice. They do this every year, even at the present time. They teach children at the present time how to do this. And any gens may do this. It is a rule.

When blueberries are ripe they do the same thing. That is how this one little act of worship is. It is for all gentes. It is strictly believed in yet. It is done every summer.

And when the corn is ripe they all have certain ways: They make Indian corn meal which is wrapped with cornstalk leaves. They boil that. This is the first little feast after the corn is ripe. And they invite six persons. And this is how the invited are seated.[2]

And this is the song they use:

I am feeding you corn;
I am feeding you corn.

---

[2] The drawing cannot be reproduced because it is partially unclear to me. What is certain is that the six invited sit in a circle on the north. Opposite them in two lines are the hummers on the south side. Two ceremonial attendants are east of the invited, one opposite the other.

This is an important way in which the people acted: In the early days when they used to have wars the men did the fighting and the women did the work at home and raised gardens. And even if the women had to go a mile or more to fetch water it was their duty to do so. And the same with respect to wood: It was their duty to get it. While they still had wars they loved their women, but to day it is not so. It is different. And this was the rule for the women: If they got up in the morning they dressed their hair before cooking. This was a strict rule. And it is still so. Young girls are taught this at the present time.

But there was one thing which was against their rules: They were not to dress in finery early in the morning. And they also taught girls the same way. The idea was not to die early. That is why they did not wear finery early in the morning. And this custom still obtains today.

And there is another strict rule which exists today: They must not whistle at night. And they still believe in this, and do not do so.

Today they act differently, but there is another thing which is strictly told to children: If anyone dies children usually get up early in the morning. This happens at the present time. Children are not allowed to sleep until the sun rises. And when anyone dies they are told not to wail. Even children are told not to bawl. And another thing: When a death occurs no drumming is to occur till 4 days have elapsed. After the fourth day they may drum all they wish.

And another thing which is strictly against their rules: They must not draw any human body on the ground. It is claimed that this is a sinful thing to do. This is one reason why they are particularly against being photographed.

And there is another thing which is against their rules: A stranger must not attend the funerals. This is a thing which was strongly believed in. This is one reason why they do not like to have white people attend their funerals; but today they think little of it. This generation is changing.

This is another thing in which they formerly believed: When people became ill they were supposed to heat a stone, dig a little hole, throw the stone in it, and lie on top of the stone. That is what they did in the early days. Once in a while they still practice it.

And this happened to women: When women lost sight of their relatives it was a strict rule for them not to cry out. They might let their tears flow. This has been told generation to generation. And so far they have kept it up. The only way that makes it possible for them to cry out is if they fast: On the fourth day they may cry out; but it must be at the grave where their relative is buried. This would happen about 3 or 4 o'clock in the morning. And this is the time they must use their songs. They do this before any of the people are awake, while everything is quiet. This is what they do. The end.

KĪ‘CE‘SŌ'GI KÄTEMINAWĀWĀᴰTCINᴺᴵ‘

Nenī'w ä‘kī'wānīᵈtc ä'‘cī‘cāᵈtc¹‘, ä‘pe‘cege‘siwe‘ci‘ᴀgᵏᴵ‘. Ä‘ᴀ‘cki'-
megu‘u'wīwiᵈtc ä‘nawänenī'‘ä‘ïᵈtc¹‘. Ī'nᴀ nā'‘k i‘kwäw ä‘wäwe'-
ne‘siᵈtc¹‘. Tcäwī‘cwi'megu ä‘wäwene'‘siwāᵈtc¹‘. Ä‘tᴀgwāgī'‘inig
ä‘uwīwe'tīwāᵈtc¹‘. Nōmᴀgä'w uwīwe'tīwāᵈtc īniᵈtcā'‘ip ä‘mawi-
5 kīwānīᵈtc¹‘. Kᴀbōtwe'megu ä‘pōnike‘kä'netᴀgi wä'ᵈtcīgwänⁿᴵ‘.
Keyä‘ᴀpᴀgä'‘ipi kī‘ce‘sōn aiyāpōtānᴀgīgwänegu'te‘e wäᵈtcipwāwi'-
meguke‘kä'netᴀgi wä'ᵈtcīgwänⁿᴵ‘. Ä‘kī‘cāguᵈtci‘tä‘äᵈtc ä‘kī'-
wānīᵈtc¹‘. Ä‘wᴀ'ni‘eᵈtc¹‘.

I‘kwä'wᴀ wänā'pämit ä‘kwä‘tāni'tä‘äᵈtc¹‘. "Ä‘cipwāwipōno-
10 wäyägwā'pe‘e wī‘menä‘cku'noyägᵏʷᵉ‘ ", ä'‘ināᵈtc ume‘sōtā'naᶜᴵ‘.
Ä‘ke‘tcine'‘ckimāᵈtc¹‘.

"Na‘i', kā'tᴀ wī'näni kīwi‘i‘ci‘i‘ci‘kāgᵏᵉ‘ ", ä'‘iguᵈtc¹‘. " ‘ᴀ'‘ce
‘i'nowäwᴀ', kī‘inänemegōpi ‘wänⁿᴬ‘. Kī‘kegyä‘tenäme‘tāgōpi'megu
ï'n ä‘ci‘i‘cimī'wägänⁿᴵ‘ ", ä'‘iguᵈtc¹‘.
15 "Meᵈtci‘iyu'gä‘ ᴀ'‘ce kete‘ci'menepʷᴬ‘ ", ä‘ināᵈtci'megu. "Īni'-
megu ä‘na‘ino'wäyägᵏʷᵉ‘ ", ä‘i‘cikī‘kī‘kimāᵈtci'megu.

Ä‘pōni'megukägō'‘i‘i'nowäᵈtci pᴀ'‘citō‘ᴬ‘. Nā‘kᴀ'ᵈtc uwī'wä‘ᴀn
ä‘ne‘ckigämoniᵈtc¹‘. "Mᴀ'nᴀ kō'‘sᴀwä'ᵈtci me‘to‘sänenī'wiyᴀnⁿᴵ‘ ",
ä'‘ināᵈtci me‘temō‘ utā'ne‘sᴀnⁿᴵ‘. "Ä‘ä'‘e", ä'‘iniᵈtc¹. "Awi-
20 tᴀgä'‘ īnᴀ kägō'‘ kī'n i‘teyᴀne kägō'‘ i‘cikä‘twäne'mene‘sᴀ ke'-
näpäm ätᴀ'megu kī'nᴀ ketä‘ci‘ᴀniwī'tᴀne'g ä‘kä‘twänegä'mo-
yᴀnⁿᴵ‘ ", ä'‘ināᵈtci metemō‘ä' utā'ne‘sᴀnⁿᴵ‘.
" ‘Kī‘tepā'netīpʷᴬ‘', kete‘cipenaiyugä'i yōwʷᵉ‘ ", ä'‘ineᵈtci
metemō‘ä‘ᴬ‘. Ä‘pōnika'nawiᵈtc ä‘ke‘tcä‘kwäniᵈtc¹‘.

25 "Kī‘pene'megu kī‘cike‘kä'nemᴀg ä‘ca'wigwäni wīᵈtca'wiwᴀgᴀ
kī‘pāpᴀgamenepwᴀ'megu tcäwī'‘cʷ¹'", ä‘i'gowāᵈtc utäne'‘-
swäwᴀnⁿᴵ‘.
Apinᴀ'megu pᴀ'‘citō‘ utō'pwāgᴀni'mō'ᴀnip ä‘wᴀ'nī‘käᵈtci
nᴀnō'‘ckw ä'‘äwāᵈtc uwī'wä‘ᴀnⁿᴵ‘.
30 Īnigä'‘ip īnᴀneni'wä‘me‘sᴀtu'nä‘uᵈtc¹‘. Änemi‘cī‘kaweᵈtci'megu
aiyä‘pī‘tcinā'‘megu ä‘ᴀnemi'ᴀ‘ka'wi‘eᵈtc¹‘. Kᴀbō'tw ä‘me'‘kᴀmeg
ä‘tᴀ'‘cine‘tawä'te‘ᵉ‘. Ä'‘näwuᵈtci pe‘cege'‘sīw ä‘ᴀ'gōᵈtcigᵏᴵ‘.
Agōnāgwä'nip¹‘. ‘Ō'nip kᴀbō'tw ä‘päwäne'mowāᵈtci nänᴀtunä'-
‘wätcigᵏᴵ‘.
35 ‘Ō'n u'wīwᴀn ä‘wäpimᴀ‘kᴀtä'wīniᵈtc¹‘. Pe‘ki'megu ä‘ke‘tcimä‘-
kᴀtä'wīᵈtc i‘kwä'wʷᴬ‘. Apinᴀ'megu ä‘ᴀ‘kᴀ'niᵈtc i‘kwä'w änᴀta-
wä'nemāᵈtc unä'pämᴀnⁿᴵ‘. Penōᵈtciyu'gä‘ ä‘inu'täwāᵈtci mᴀmänō-
gu'nip ä'gwi wī‘se'niᵈtcinⁿᴵ‘. Ä‘kī‘cāguᵈtcitcāgi'ᵈtciniᵈtc ᴀ'‘saiyᴀn
ukōtä‘ upī'‘se‘ka‘i nā'‘k īni'megu ä‘tcāgi'tenig ᴀ‘saiyipī'‘se‘kaᶜᴵ‘.
40 ‘Ō'nipi kᴀbō'tw ä‘ke‘kä'nemāᵈtci kᴀtawi. "Āgwi'ku‘
nepō'‘iᵈtcini ke'näpämᵐᴬ‘ ", ä'‘ineᵈtc ä‘inā'‘pᴀ'wāᵈtc¹‘. Ä‘inä-

THE ONE WHOM THE MOONS BLESSED

A man was lost when hunting, when hunting deer. He had just been married and he was a fine-looking man. And the woman was beautiful. Both were beautiful. It was in the fall when they married. When they had been married a short time then it is said he went out and was lost. Soon he ceased to know whence he had come. It is a fact, so it is said, that the reason why he did not know whence he had come was because his eyes had been turned upside down by the moon. He felt terribly when he was lost. He was missed.

The woman whose husband he was felt sorrowful. "It is because you never have ceased saying that you desired fresh meat", she said to her parents. She scolded them severely.

"Now do not go about saying that of us", she was told. "You will not be thought like this, 'she is just saying so.' It will be thought that you are telling the truth when you say that of us", she was told.

"Well, I am not lying about you any way", she said to them. "That indeed is what you have kept on saying", she insisted on telling them.

The old man ceased saying anything. And his wife scolded. "This your father is why you are a human being", the old woman said to her daughter. "Yes", the latter said. "Your husband would not have grieved over you if something had happened to you, while you go on terribly in grieving," the little old woman said to her daughter.

"Yet you formerly told us, 'Be fond of each other' ", the little old woman was told. She ceased speaking, as her daughter was very angry.

"If I ever find out what has happened to the one with whom I live (i. e., husband) I shall club you both to death", they were told by their daughter.

The old man even forgot his tobacco pouch when he and his wife went away, not knowing where.

Then, it is said, everyone searched for that man. He was trailed, and once in a while they found his trail. Soon they found where he had killed game. A deer was seen suspended. For, it is said, he had hung it up. And, it is said, the searchers soon became discouraged.

Then his wife began to fast. The woman fasted very earnestly. The woman even became skinny, as she desired her husband. While they were moving far off she did not eat for several days. Her buckskin skirt was all torn and her buckskin waist also was all torn.

And, it is said, soon she almost found out about him. "Your husband is not dead", she was told in a dream. She told those whose

ᵈtci'mo'ā̆ᵈtci   wägwi'si'niᵈtci'i   nāpi'megu   ä'kīgina'wämā̆ᵈtcⁱᶜ.
'Ō'nipⁱᶜ, "Ä'cawigwä'ni'ckwe", ä'ci'tä'ä̆ᵈtc i'kwä'wʷᴬᶜ.

KАbō'twe nā̆''kᴀ pe'ki'megu ä'kī'cāguᵈtcike'sī'yänigi nā̆''inā̆'ⁱᶜ,
"Mᴀɴᴀ''kāni wī''aiyᴀnⁿⁱᶜ ", ä''ineᵈtc ä'inā̆''pᴀ'wā̆ᵈtcⁱᶜ.   Wätutä'-
5 wāte'ᵉᶜ.   "Kī''näwāwʷᴬᶜ: wīᵈtca'wiwᴀt īyā̆'ᶜ u'wīgīwʷᴬᶜ ", ä''ineᵈtc
ä'inā̆''pᴀ'wā̆ᵈtcⁱᶜ.

Wīɴᴀgä''ⁱ īɴᴀ nenī'w īyā̆'ᶜ ä'u'wīgiᵈtc ä'awiwā̆'te'ᵉᶜ.   Wīɴᴀgä''ⁱ
īn i'kwä'w īte'p ä'ā̆'ᵈtci penōᵈtci'megu.   KАbō'tw ä'keᵈtcīᵈtci
wäᵈtcīwā̆'te' ä'pemā̆'kwaiyä''inigᵏⁱᶜ.
10 Pe'kigä''megu ä'kī'cāguᵈtci'meguke'sī'yänigᵏⁱᶜ. Ä''nätᴀg äyā̆ᵈtc
ä'pege''cänigᵏⁱᶜ.   "Ī'ni", ä'ci'tä'ä̆ᵈtc ä'mī'cātā'nemuᵈtcⁱᶜ: änemi'-
cine''kyänig ä'ᴀne'mi'ā̆ᵈtcⁱᶜ.

'Ō'nipi pe'ku'tänig īte'p ä'ā̆'ᵈtcⁱᶜ, kīmō'ᵈtc ä'wā̆'pᴀmā̆ᵈtc
unāpämᴀnі'ᵈtcā̆ᶜ   ä'tᴀ'cinᴀ'sā̆'kō'i'gäniᵈtcⁱᶜ.   Ä'pe'mipī'tigäᵈtci
15 nenī'w īni'n aiyōninä̆'ᶜ u'wīwᴀn ä''näwā̆ᵈtcⁱᶜ.   Ä'wī'cā'penä̆ᵈtc
i'kwä'w ä'ᴀ'cᴀ'meguᵈtci kākī'ce'sᴀ'miniᵈtci menā̆''ckunōnⁿⁱᶜ.

'Ō'nipⁱᶜ, "Täniᵈtcā̆' ä'ciwäpike'käne'miyᴀn aiyō̆' ä'a'wiyänⁿⁱᶜ ",
ä''ineᵈtc i'kwä'wʷᴬᶜ.

"Ä'mᴀ'kᴀtäwīyäniᵈtcā̆''ⁱᶜ ", ä'i''ciwäᵈtcⁱᶜ.
20 Wā̆'pᴀnigᵏⁱᶜ, "Na'ī' pe'ki'megu wī'na''awinwi," ä'i'ᵈtci nenī'wʷᴬᶜ.
Īni'megu ä'i''cikeg ä'na''awigᵏⁱᶜ.   'Ō'nip ä'pe'nowā̆ᵈtc ai'yāpᴀm
ä''āwā̆ᵈtcⁱᶜ. Apinᴀ'megu i'kwä'w ä'pwāwike'kä'netᴀgi wī'i'ci'aiyī-
'kwigwänⁿⁱᶜ. Ä'ke'ci'gīwā̆ᵈtciyu'gä̆'ⁱᶜ. Änawä'nemä̆ᵈtc unā̆'pämᴀn
ä'myä'ci''säniᵈtcⁱᶜ. A'ckᴀ'ᵈtci tepe''kīnig ä''pyāwā̆ᵈtci wäᵈtcīᵈtc
25 i'kwäw ä'uwī'giwā̆ᵈtc i'kwäw ä'ne'pāwā̆ᵈtcⁱᶜ.

Wā̆pᴀnig ä'näwāwā̆ᵈtci kä''kyä'ᴀg unegwᴀ'nwāwᴀn ä'mi'cätäne'-
mowā̆ᵈtcⁱᶜ.

'Ō'nip īte'p ä''āwā̆ᵈtci nenī'w ume'sō'tänä̆ᶜ ä'a'winiᵈtcⁱᶜ.
Ō'sᴀ'ni nä'wuguᵈtc ä'nᴀgᴀpe'kwä''säniᵈtcⁱᶜ. Kī'ci'meguna'itä-
30 'äniᵈtcⁱᶜ, "Na'ī', ä'upiyäpᴀni'megunä'wutīg ä'cime'nwikegᵏⁱᶜ.
Īni'megu me''tenō̆'ⁱᶜ. Mᴀ'ni wī'n ä'cᴀ'kwinäwutīgin ä̆'gwi
na'i'keginⁿⁱᶜ. Ä'äni'äni'gowäg ī'ni me'nwikegᵏⁱᶜ ", ä''inā̆ᵈtc ō'sᴀ'nⁿⁱᶜ.
"Nī'naiyō̆' na''ina'i kīwā̆'nīyäni nekī'cāguᵈtci'tä'ᵉᶜ. 'Wä'gunä'i
wī'mīᵈtcīwänänⁿⁱᶜ? Ke'känetᴀmō̆'iyäni pe'ki'megu nekī'cāgutᴀ-
35 'pene.   Mō̆'tci'megu ne'pi netᴀ'gäwätᴬᶜ.   'Nī'nepō̆'i'megu',
nete'ci'tä'ᵉᶜ.

"Me'cemegō̆'na'i ne'gutä̆' ä'cegi'cegi''cinän ätᴀ'megu nemen-
wimenwi'cinⁿᵉᶜ. KАbōtwä̆' īn ä'pyäᵈtcipᴀ'gi'cigi wī'ckenō̆'ä'ᴀ
mī'ci'tepäwâpᴀtä'nīwʷᴬᶜ. ' "Nete'pänetᴀ nīya'wi", kete'citä'ᵉᶜ?'
40 nete'gᵏʷᴬᶜ. 'Penᴀ wâpᴀminu", nete'gᵏʷᴬᶜ. Ī'n ä'wā̆'pᴀmᴀgᵏⁱᶜ.
Īniᵈtcā̆' änäpᴀmᴀgi mᴀ'n änā̆ᵈtci'moyänⁿⁱᶜ. Tō̆'kīyän īni nemen-
wipemāte'sⁱᶜ. Ke'yä'ᴀpᴀgä''i nepai'yäne'ᵉᶜ. 'Wägunä ī'niy
ä'cäwe''siyänⁿⁱᶜ? Wänᴀtō̆'kᴀ'megu nepī'nō̆'sōwʷⁱᶜ. Nemī'cätä-
nemᵐᵘᶜ. 'Īni'ku'i', nete''citä̆' ä''näwᴀgi kī'ce''sʷᴬᶜ. Nekī'ciyu'-
45 gä'imō̆''ci'āwᴀ.   Pe'kutägᵏⁱᶜ ᴀpinᴀ'megu ä'wâwâ'sinī'gwᴀtäg

son he was, and made them feel somewhat better. Then, it is said, the woman thought, "I wonder what has happened to him, by gad?"

And soon when it was very cold she was told in her dream, "You will go yonder." It was where they had moved from. "You will see him: the one you live with (i. e., husband) dwells yonder", she was told in her dream.

And the man lived yonder whither they were going. And the woman went thither (but) far off. Soon she came in sight of whence they had come, where a little forest was.

It was very, very cold. Where she was going she saw smoke. "That is it", she thought and rejoiced: she went along where she could not be seen.

And, it is said, at night she went there and secretly indeed saw her husband as he was broiling meat on spits. The man started to walk in when he saw his wife before him. As she was hungry the woman was fed the fresh meat which he had cooked.

And, it is said, the woman was asked, "How did you know that I was staying here?"

"Because I fasted", she said.

The next day the man said, "Well, it will be warm."

It was so; it was warm. Then, it is said, they departed and went back. The woman did not even know that she was tired. Yet they were going on speedily. She thought her husband was not fast enough, as he was slow. Later on they came at night whence the woman had come and they slept where they stayed.

The next day the old folks saw their son-in-law and were glad.

And, it is said, they went where the man's parents dwelt. When he was seen by his father, the latter hung his head. After the latter felt easier, he said to his father, "Well, to see each other in good humor is very good. It is the only way. But this, seeing each other in a drowzy way, is not good. Saying funny things is good. As for me, when I was lost I felt terribly. What, pray, was there for me to eat? When I regained consciousness I was terribly hungry. I even desired water. 'I shall indeed die', I thought.

"When I was lying down somewhere, I lay down comfortably. Soon then a little bird who seemed to have a fuzzy crest on its head came and alit. 'Do you think, "I own myself?" ' it said to me. 'Please look at me', it said to me. And I looked at it. When I looked at it it was exactly as I have said. As soon as I woke up, I felt as well as possible. It is a fact that I had slept. Where was the hunger I had felt? I felt healthy, without a care. I was proud. 'That's it', I thought as I saw the moon. For I had had a vision of it. The night was so cold it even sparkled. And I knew what the

ä‘kī‘cāguᵈtcike‘sītepe‘kīgᵏⁱᶜ.   Neke‘kä′nemāwᴀgigä′näpe‘ ä‘ciwī′-
‘sowāᵈtci kī′‘ce‘sōgᵏⁱᶜ′′′, ä′‘ināᵈtc ō‘sᴀ′nⁿⁱᶜ. “ ‘Ō′, ‘ō′′′, ä′‘iguᵈtcⁱᶜ.

“Tᴀgwᴀtä′‘ᴬ‘: ī′n (A ki to le) ä‘ā′mī‘ā′mīᵈtci me‘to‘sä′nenīwᵂᴬ‘.
Īnigä′‘ ä‘tᴀgwᴀ′tᴀgwᴀgᵏⁱᶜ.

5   “Wäpenāwikī‘ce′‘sᵂᴬ‘ (No le no le): ī′n äwäpipepōgᵏⁱᶜ: ä‘wäpi′-
megu‘ᴀgo‘ᴀgōnī‘kīwigᵏⁱᶜ.

“ ‘Ō′ni Ke‘tcimᴀ‘kwikī‘ce′‘sᵂᴬ‘ (Ti se mi le): ī′ni pe‘ki′megu
ä‘ke‘sike′‘siyāgᵏⁱᶜ.

“Tcᴀgimᴀ‘kwikī′‘ce‘sō′‘ᴬ‘ (Tte ni we): ī′ni pe′‘k ä‘wī‘sᴀwī‘sᴀge′-
10 ‘siyāgᵏⁱᶜ; ä‘kutᴀᵈtcimeᵈtci mᴀ‘kwipᴀnᴀ′cā′‘ä‘ᴀgᵏⁱᶜ.

“ ‘Ō′ni Tcāgä′nemetᴀ‘ (Se lo we, Sepowä′‘ᴀ): nōtä′gi‘itᴀ‘
ä‘ᴀ‘swänemeguᵈtci manetowa‘ⁱᶜ. Īni wä′ᵈtci te′‘kā‘suᵈtci ‘Tᴀg-
wᴀnī′‘ᴀ′ ä‘tᴀgwᴀnīgᵏⁱᶜ. Īni nā′‘k äyīg uwī‘sōnⁿⁱᶜ.

“ ‘Ō′ni Pāpō‘kwī‘ᴀ (Ma tta, Māᵈtc‘ᴬ‘): pāpō′‘kwīni wī′na′‘awigᵏⁱᶜ.
15 Ī′ni wä′ᵈtci te′‘kā‘suᵈtcⁱᶜ.

“ ‘Ō′ni Pā′pᴀ‘kwā′ᴀ (Īpᴀ′nⁿᴬ‘, I la na): me‘tegō′n ī′ni wī′pᴀ′-
‘kwᴀnīgᵏⁱᶜ. Me‘to‘säne′niwᴀg ī′n ä‘ᴀnegä‘kō‘käwāᵈtcⁱᶜ, ä‘ᴀ‘ci′gä-
wāᵈtc uwīge′wāwᴀnⁿⁱᶜ.

“ ‘Ō′n Āpāmi′ne‘kä′ᴀ (Mī‘ᴬ‘, Mi ᴀ): āmi‘āmītcig īn ä‘pōnipōnī-
20 wāᵈtci me‘to‘sänéniwᴀgᵏⁱᶜ.

“ ‘Ō′n A‘ki‘käwikī‘ce′‘swᴀ (Tcō′nⁿᴬ‘, Tto na): ä ‘ᴀ‘ki‘ᴀ‘ki′‘kä-
wāᵈtci me‘to‘säne′niwᴀgᵏⁱᶜ. Ī′ni wäᵈtc i‘cite′‘kā‘suᵈtcⁱᶜ, änegwᴀ-
ᵈtci‘ᴀ′mowā tc utᴀ‘kī′wāwᴀnⁿⁱᶜ.

“ ‘Ō′ni Penā′wikī‘ce′‘swᴀ (Tcōnai′ʸᴬ‘, Tto na ya): Nāwipenā′-
25 wikī‘ce′‘sᵂᴬ‘, ä‘nāwipenāwi′gᵏⁱᶜ.

“ ‘Ō′ni Nīpenikī‘ce′‘swᴀ (Āgi‘st‘ᴬ‘, A ki sta): ī′n ä′‘nīpegᵏⁱᶜ.
Ī′n ä‘tcāgi′megunīpe′gᵏⁱᶜ, tcā′gi kägō′‘ ī′n ä‘kī‘cimämäᵈtciwikī′-
‘cikegᵏⁱᶜ.

“ ‘Ō′n Āmᴀnowikī‘ce′‘swᴀ (Sepite′mipä‘ᴬ‘, Se li te mi le): īn
30 ä‘āmᴀnowāᵈtci pe‘cege′‘siwᴀgᵏⁱᶜ.

“ ‘Ī′n ä‘ci‘cite‘kā′‘sowāᵈtcⁱᶜ.

“Wī‘sᴀ‘kä‘ ä‘tᴀnwäwä′tīwāᵈtci manetowᴀni wī‘tᴀ‘ci′nigwäni kī′-
‘ce‘sō‘ⁱᶜ.   ‘Ō′ni manetōwᵂᴬ‘, ‘mᴀ′nᴀ wī‘āwᴀgᴀ penä′wᵂᴬ‘’, ä‘ci-
wäᵈtcipⁱᶜ.

35   “ ‘Ō′n penä′w ä‘nene‘ckigäᵈtcä‘ckäᵈtcⁱᶜ.

“ ‘Ä‘tᴀ‘switcītīyäᵈtci wī‘tᴀ′‘ciniᵈtci kī′‘ce‘sō‘ⁱᶜ.’

“Penä′w ä‘pyäᵈtcitīyägäpäᵈtcⁱᶜ.

“ ‘Agime′‘kōnigᵏⁱᶜ’, ä‘i′‘ciwäᵈtcⁱᶜ, ‘uᵈtcītīyä‘ⁱᶜ. Negu‘ti penä′we
ī′ni wī‘tᴀ′‘ciwäᵈtci pepō′ge īni′megu wī‘tᴀ‘ciwäᵈtcⁱᶜ’, ä‘i′‘ciwäᵈtcⁱᶜ.
40   “ ‘Āgwikᴀnā′gᵏʷᴬ‘, ä‘i′‘ciwäᵈtci Wī′‘sᴀ‘kä‘ᴬ‘.

“ ‘Īnimā′‘megu ä‘kī‘cäwīyᴀgᵏʷᵉᵗ’, ä‘i′‘ciwäᵈtci manetōw äne′tᴀ‘.

moons (months) were called", he said to his father. "Oh yes", he was told.

"TᴀgwᴀtäꞋꞋᴀ (October): then is when the people move away. It is then fall.

"Wäpenāwi-month (November): then it begins to be winter; there indeed begins to be permanent snow on the ground.

"And the Great Bear month (KeꞋtcimᴀꞋkwi-, December): then it is very cold.

"The Little Bear month (TcᴀgimᴀꞋkwi-, January): then one suffers from the cold; the young bears are tested.

"And Opposed By All (Tcāgänemetᴀ, February): it is one which is short (in the number of days) as it is opposed by the manitous. That is why it is called 'TᴀgwᴀnīꞋᴀ' (Hard Crust), because there is hard crust on the snow. That also is its name.

"And Half and Half (PāpōꞋkwīꞋᴀ, March): It will be warm part of the time. That is why it is so called.

"Then Bark Works Out (PāpᴀꞋkwäꞋᴀ, April): Then the bark may be peeled from trees. Then the people seek barks and build their dwellings.

"Then ĀpāmineꞋkäꞋᴀ (May): Then the people who had moved away camp (i. e., settle in their summer quarters).

"Then Farming-month (AꞋkiꞋkäwi-, June): Then the people farm. That is why it is so called, because they hoe their lands.

"Then Summer-month (Penāwi-, July): It is Middle of Summer Month when it is the middle of summer.

"Then Harvest-month (Nīpeni-, August): Then it is harvest. Then everything is harvested, then everything has matured.

"Then Rutting month (ĀmᴀnowikīꞋceswᴀ, September): Then the deer rut.

"That is how they are called.

"WiꞋsᴀꞋkäꞋᴀ and a manitou were quarreling as to how many months (moons) there should be. And the manitou said, it is said, 'I shall use this turkey.'

"Now a turkey stood there with its tail spread.

" 'The months will be the number of its tail feathers.'

"The turkey came, standing with its tail (spread).

" 'Count these tail feathers', he said, 'In one summer there will be just as many (months) and in winter just as many', he said.

" 'No indeed', said WiꞋsꞋAkaꞋᴀ.

" 'We have now already made our plans', said the one called 'a manitou.'

" 'Ā'gwi', ä'i'ᶜciwäᵈtci Wī'ᶜsA'kä'ᴬᶜ. 'Nī'nAkuᵈtci nī'ᶜäᵈtci-
mᵐᵘᶜ', ä'i'ᶜciwäᵈtcⁱᶜ. 'Kīnaiyu'mAni kī'ᶜäᵈtcimu wä'ᵈtci wī'mā-
näwäᵈtc i'citä'ä'wAnänⁿⁱᶜ'.

" "Ō' nī'äᵈtcimᵐᵘᶜ', ä'i'ᶜciwäᵈtci ma'netōwᵂᴬᶜ. 'Me'ce'megu
5 kīkīwītāwā'sA penä'winigᵏᵉᶜ; pe'pōnige me'ce'megu tA'cimāmA-
'kAtäwīwā's'ᴬᶜ', ä'i'ᶜciwäᵈtcⁱᶜ, 'Anemime'to'säne'niwAgᵏⁱᶜ. Īni nīnA
wī'mā'näwäᵈtci wä'ᵈtc i'citä'ᶜäyäni kī'ᶜce'sōgᵏⁱᶜ', ä'ᶜineᵈtci Wī'-
'sA'kä'ᴬᶜ. Īn ä'ᶜineᵈtcⁱᶜ. 'Wä'ᵈtci "Kekī'cä'wīpenⁿᴬᶜ" 'i'nenänⁿⁱᶜ',
ä'ᶜineᵈtci Wī'ᶜsA'kä'ᴬᶜ.

10 " 'Ōnipⁱᶜ, 'nīnA nā'ᶜkāni wī'ke'käne'miyAn ä'citä'ᶜäyänⁿⁱᶜ.
Āgwigä'ᶜ ä'cimyā'netegi wī'ine'nänini nī'nⁿᴬᶜ. Ä'ci'megumenwi'ge-
nigi netenä'nemäw Anemime'to'säneniwᵂᴬᶜ. A'ce' mAni nī'n
ä'tcīna'wämAg ī'ni wä'ᵈtc ä'cimenwi'genig inänemAgᵏⁱᶜ.
Kwāgwinō'A' mAnA. AgitAmu'gu tA'se'nwi ketAgi'sigiwäyäni:
15 wī'tA'ᶜciwäᵈtci negu'ti penä'wᵂᵉᶜ', ä'i'ᶜciwäᵈtcⁱᶜ. 'Inimä'ᶜ kīnⁿᴬᶜ.
Ke'tenA' mAnA täpwä'wᵂᴬᶜ. Negu'ti me'tciyäwe ku'twā'cigA
'ō'ni negu'ti pepō'nwe ku'twā'cigᵏᴬᶜ. 'Ō'ni negu'ti ke'kA'twe 'i'ni
medā'ᶜswi nī'ᶜcwi wī'tA'ciwäᵈtci kī'ᶜce'sōgᵏⁱᶜ; menwitA'ᶜsw īnⁿⁱᶜ.
Ke'tenA'megu ä'pī'ᶜtcikeg ī'ni ne'ᶜki wī'pemipäpenäwigᵏⁱᶜ. 'Ō'ni
20 me'toᵈtci'megu nōmAgäwe wī'ᶜpepōgᵏⁱᶜ. Āgwi'kägō'i wī'kī'ci'kegini
pepō'gᵏᵉᶜ. Nā'ᶜkA me'ᶜsōtäw uwī'yä'ä'A wī'ne'pAᵈtcīwᵂᴬᶜ. Wī'cäg-
wänemōwAᵈtcä'i kenwä'ᶜci wī'pe'pōnigᵏⁱᶜ. Ke'sī'yänige mäne'megu
tcāgAᵈtci'ᶜs'ᴬᶜ. Ī'ni wī'nA nänōmAgäwe'megu pe'pōnigᵏᵉᶜ, me'ceme-
gō'na' uwī'yä'ä'A tätäpA'kwipemeneti'su'sA näne'kA'nipepō'nᵂᵉᶜ.
25 Ī'ni wī'nA mänäni'te pepōnikī'ᶜce'sō'i mägwä'megu awi't u'wīyä'A
tAgu'ᶜsA nAnō'ᵈtci kīwītä'ä'A nAnō'ᵈtci mī'ᵈtcipä'ᴬᶜ. MA'nA nā'ᶜk
Anemime'to'sä'neniw ini'megu āmi'ᶜcawiᵈtcⁱᶜ. Wī'mīᵈtciᵈtci
wī'kī'ci'setäti'suᵈtci me'cemegōna'i kägō'ᶜⁱᶜ. Ī'n ä'cinīnAtä'pwä-
yänⁿⁱᶜ. Ī'ni', ä'ᶜineᵈtci ma'netōwᵂᴬᶜ.

30 "Mänäni 'īn ä'i'cimenwä'netAgi ma'netōw änäwe'niwitᴬᶜ.
" 'Īnī'ku' ä'cime'nwikegi mA'nⁿⁱᶜ', inä'ᵈtcimōwᵂᴬᶜ.

"Īn ä'cike'kä'nemAgᵏⁱᶜ, Anō'ᶜs'ᵉᶜ; ī'ni pyäᵈtcinäᵈtci'moyäni
me'tōᵈtci'megu kenä'tA pyäᵈtcinäᵈtcimo'ᶜenän aiyäpōtänAgī-
gwä'igigä'ᶜⁱᶜ. Kī'ᶜce'sōgi kī'ci'aiyäᵈtcimo'ᶜiwäᵈtc ī'n ä'näyäpänAgī'-
35 gwänigᵏⁱᶜ, ä'ke'känetAmän ä'kīwä'nīyän ä'pe'noyänⁿⁱᶜ. Ī'n ä'ca'wi-
yän änäᵈtcimo'ᶜenänⁿⁱᶜ, Anō'ᶜsᵉᶜ. Ī'n ä'kwi'ᵈtcⁱᶜ'', ä'ᶜineᵈtci
pA'ᶜcitō'ᴬᶜ.

" 'No', said Wīʻsaʻkäʻa. 'For I shall have something to say', he said. 'And you will have to explain why you desire (the months) to be so many.'

" 'Oh, I shall explain', said the manitou. 'In summer they might simply live peacefully; and in winter the future people might fast', he said, 'That is why I desired the months to be many', Wīʻsaʻkäʻa was told. So he was told. 'It is why I told you, "We have already made our plans" ' ', Wīʻsaʻkäʻa was told.

"Then, it is said, 'Now you may learn what I think. I shall not say anything evil to you. I wish the future people what is good. Simply because I am related to them is why I wish them what is good. This is a chipmunk. Count how many stripes there are on its back: (the months) will be so many in one summer', he said. 'Now you have it. This one certainly tells the truth. In one summer there will be 6 and in one winter there will be 6. And in 1 year there will be 12 months; that is a good number. Surely indeed as many as that it will continue to be summer. And it seems as if it would be winter (but) a short time. Nothing will mature in winter. And every little thing will be cold. It will be unwilling indeed for it to be winter very long. If it were cold many might entirely freeze. Now if it were winter for a very short time, then anyone might take care of himself throughout the whole winter. Now if there were many months of winter perhaps no game animal would be plentiful nor in existence. The same thing would happen to this, the future people. They would have to store away anything to eat. That is the truth I tell. That is all', the manitou was told.

"Many a one called a manitou favored it.

" 'That indeed is the best way', he said.

"That is what I know of him, father; it seems as if you had seen what I have narrated and my eyes were turned upside down as I have narrated. As soon as the moons (months) instructed me then they turned my eyes right side up, and when I regained consciousness I was lost and came home. I experienced what I have told you, father. That is all", the old man was told.

LINGUISTIC NOTES ON THE INDIAN TEXT

There has been so much discussion of Fox linguistics that it is only necessary to translate a few words, and to add a grammatical note in order to make the Indian text intelligible to the professional student: AgitAmu'gu count them (inan.).   74.14.

Agime''kōnig^{klᵗ} count them (an.; contraction of Agime'ku and īnig^{klᵗ}).   72.38.   (Agi count; m-intsr. with animate, -t instr. with inanimate object.)

ä'amAnowā^{d}ci when they rut.   72.30.   (Stem āmAno- rut, be lustful; not āmAnowi- as given by me previously; -wi- [-w-] is the element discussed by me on several occasions.)

ä'Aswänemegu^{d}tci is opposed by.   72.12.   (The initial stem is A'sw-; -äne- is well known; compare Cree Aswēyimēw, he guards against him.)

ä'Anegä'kō'käwā^{d}tc^{lᵗ} they seek bark.   72.17.   (-'kä- is the common auxiliary.)

ä'Anemi'A'ka'wi'e^{d}tc^{lᵗ} they continued to trail him.   68.31.   (Anemi- to continue;   A'kawi- to pursue.)

ä'äni'äni'gowäg(i) when funny things are said.   70.32.   (See änigi- funny, p. 627, Fortieth Ann. Rept. Bur. Amer. Ethn.; the combination of this and -wä- sound, yield änigowä-; strictly, the chronology is pre-Fox.)

ä'upiyāpAni'megunäwutīg(i) seeing each other in good humor.   70.30.   (upiyāni is clearly connected in some way with upi- happy.)

ä'ke'ci'gīwā^{d}tciyu'gä'i yet they were going along speedily.   70.23.   (Cf. p. 632, Fortieth Ann. Rept. Bur. Amer. Ethn.; also p. 180, Bull. 105, Bur. Amer. Ethn.)

ä'kī'cāgu^{d}tcike'sītepe'kīg^{klᵗ} the night was very cold.   72.1.   (Purely rhetorical for ke'si-.)

ä'kī'cimämä^{d}tciwikī'cikī'cikeg^{klᵗ} it has certainly matured.   72.27, 28.   (mämä^{d}tci certainly?)

ä'kutA^{d}tcime^{d}tci they are tested with cold.   72.10.   (The first stem is ku- try, test, with postverbal -t- -^{d}tci-; the second stem is -A- cold, with postverbal -t- -^{d}tci-; cf. nepA^{d}tci- be chilly, sīgA^{d}tci- freeze, tcāgA^{d}tci- be entirely frozen, etc.)

ä'kwä'tāni'tä'ä^{d}tc^{lᵗ} she felt sorrowful.   68.9.   (The first stem is kwä'tän-.)

ä'tAgwA'tAgwAg^{klᵗ} it is then fall.   72.4.   (It is obvious that tAgwägi- be fall is related in some way.)

ä'tAgwAnīg^{klᵗ} there is frost with a hard crust.   72.13.

ä'tA'cinA'sä'kō'i'gäni^{d}tc^{lᵗ} he was there broiling on a spit.   70.14.   (Compare äna'sä'kuhäwätc[1] they roasted his flesh on the spit, Jones' Fox Texts, 92.5.)

ä'tA'cine'tawä'te'e^ᵗ where he had killed game.   68.32.   (For ne'tawä- see Fortieth Ann. Rept. Bur. Amer. Ethn., p. 289.)

Ä'tA'switcītīyä^dtc as many tail feathers as it has. 72.36.

ä'nAgApe'kwä''sāni^dtc^{ıᵗ} he dropped his head. 70.29. (Compare nAgApe'kwäpi-, p. 642, Fortieth Ann. Rept. Bur. Amer. Ethn.; and ä'nAgAnīgwä'sā^dtc^{ıᵗ} he dropped his eyelashes.)

ä'pe'cege'siwe'Ag^{kıᵗ} he was hunting deer. 68.1. (Of similar construction is ä'mA'kwe''ci'Agi he was hunting bears; pe'cege'sīwA deer, mA'kwA bear; presumably the same as -e'ci- chase, with -'w- instr. for animate object and -'- for inanimate object; probably intransitive -e'ci- in ä'tAgwāge''ciwä^dtc^{ıᵗ} they were camping in the fall [for which cognates exist in other Algonquian languages] is related.)

ä'pemā'kwaiyä''inigi where there was a little forest. 70.9. (The form is a rhetorical one, and an obviative; the evidence of Ojibwa makes this clear; see also §18 of the Algonquian sketch, Bull. 40, pt. 1, Bur. Amer. Ethn.)

ä'myā'ci'sāni^dtc^{ıᵗ} he was slow. 70.24. (The literal meaning would be, he ran badly; a specialized meaning is to be seen in myā'ci'säwi it lacks a keen edge; the stems have been explained.)

ä'wâwâ'sinīgwAtäg it sparkled; it shone like an eye (?) 70.45. (This establishes wâ'si-, not wâ'se-, as the principal stem; for the rest note PA'citōnīgwA Old Eye, a personal name.)

ä'wäpi'megu'Ago'Agōni'kīwig^{kıᵗ} there begins to be permanent snow on the ground. 72.5, 6. (Notice that we have a reduplication that belongs in §25 of the Algonquian sketch; see Agōni and -'ki-, pp. 624 and 635, Fortieth Ann. Rept. Bur. Amer. Ethn.; cf. also AgōnA snow.)

ä'wī'sAwī'sAge''siyäg^{kıᵗ} one suffers from the cold. 72.9, 10. (We have a case of reduplication which belongs in §25 of the Algonquian sketch; wī'sAgi- and ke'siyägi are combined with haplology.)

Änawä'nemā^dtc she objected to him (?). 70.23. (The word is translated on the basis of Ojibwa nindānawänimā I object to him.)

änegwA^dtci'A'mowä^dtc they were hoeing them. 72.22, 23. (Since my notes give inegwA^dtci'Amōgi, än- must be read; the evidence of Ojibwa, however, points distinctly to ä'n-.)

änemi'cine''kyänig where she could not be seen. 70.11, 12. (The translation is one of convenience; the stems Anemi-, i'ci-, ne'kī- are clear enough; we have a rather peculiar composition of ne'kī- and the inanimate copula -yā-.)

änemi'cī'kawe^dtci he was trailed. 68.30. (The translation is one of convenience; the stems Anemi-, i'ci-, and the instr. -'kaw- are easily recognized.)

u^dtcītīyä'^{ıᵗ} his tail feathers. 72.38. (My notes are insufficient to elucidate the syntactic and morphological peculiarities. [Cf. -tīyä-rump, tail.])

aiyāpōtānAgīgwänegu'te'e his eyes had been turned upside down by. 68.6.

aiyāpōtānAgīgwä'igigä'i my eyes were turned upside down. 74.33, 34. (This and the preceding word may be considered together: aiyāpōt- is a reduplication of āpōt- for which see p. 623, Fortieth Ann. Rept. Bur. Amer. Ethn.; the Cree correspondent to the latter, with the same instrumentals, has an apparently more specialized meaning; incidentally it may be added that the t is presumably postverbal, and not an integral portion of the stem.)

ketAgi'sigiwäyäni stripes on the back. 74.14. (My notes do not eluci- date the posterior portion; note however ketAgikä'kä'A striped breast.)

ketAniwī'tAneg(u) you carry on so. 68.21. (This is purely rhetorical for ketAniwi-; the stems are aniwi- and tAnego-.)

tcāgAᵈtci'sA' he might entirely freeze. 74.23. (See under ä'kutAᵈt- cimeᵈtci.)

tAgu'sA he, she would be plentiful. 74.26. (The translation is based on Poweshiek's paraphrase and the evidence of Cree and Ojibwa; apparently related to tAgwi-.)

ä'nene'ckigäᵈtcä'ckäᵈtcⁱᵗ it stood with its tail spread. 72.35. (The medial portion is unclear; ne'cki- spread, -'ckä-, -'ckä- is the com- mon auxiliary.)

nōtä'gi'itA' short in numbers. 72.11. (Translated on the basis of Cree nō'tē- deficient, short of, Ojibwa nōndä- deficient, short of; also my own notes support the meaning; the posterior portion needs no elucidation.)

pāpō''kwīni half and half. 72.14. (This is a compound of pāpō'kwi and īni; pāpō'kwi is a reduplication of pō'kwi-; for the specialized meaning of the latter compare the personal name Pō'kwimA'wäwA Half-Wolf.)

me'tciyäwe the warm half of a year. 74.16.

mī'cī'tepäwâpAtānīwᵂᴬ' it (an.) seemed fuzzy on its head. 70.39. (Purely rhetorical for mī'ci-.)

wī'na''awinwi it will be warm. 70.20. (For convenience wī'na'- 'awigᵏⁱ', 72.14, it will be warm, ä'na''awigᵏⁱ' it was warm, 70.21, are listed here; the loss of terminal n before -gi is because original -nk- becomes -g- in Fox; my notes indicate äw as opposed to aw of the text.)

wī'pA''kwAnīgᵏⁱ' the bark may be peeled from. 72.16, 17. (Ojibwa indicates pA'kwān- as opposed to the text.)

The text at 74.26 contains a wholly anomalous form kiwītä'ä'A which must be a potential subjunctive as it is coordinate with tAgu'sA. In rather vague way it recalls the none too clear potential subjunctive in -nä'A. (See Bull. 72, Bur. Amer. Ethn., p. 70; Bull. 95, Bur. Amer. Ethn., p. 39; Fortieth Ann. Rept. Bur. Amer. Ethn., pp. 287, 347, 349, 494).

The combination mānäni at 74.30 is simply māne+īni.

WHEN THE WAR CHIEFS WORSHIP THE WOLF

SECTION 1

Now the one who was blessed was Kepäyōmāwᴀ who was a member of the War Chiefs gens. This is what happened to him. When he first began to think of himself (he realized that) he was wretched. "How, pray, may I learn something?" he thought when a boy. From then on he began to carefully examine himself, and he thought about all his relatives, and his chiefs, and the children, and finally all the people. Verily at that time he thought of the Spirit of Fire. "This, probably, is how I might learn about my life", he thought. And so, it seems, he started to pick up ashes, and gave the Spirit of Fire a smoke of tobacco, and he began to tell the Spirit of Fire how he felt that he was wretched and all the reasons why he went about wailing. After, it seems, he had told him all that he felt, then, it seems, he started to go out, and went about wailing. He wailed toward the east. At night he came back. And in the morning he wailed toward the south; and at night he came back. Thereupon the next day he walked to the west and went about wailing continuously; and at night he came back. Thereupon the next day he went to the north, and he wailed all day. And all the time he did not eat. He spoke all the time for 4 days, and for as many days he spoke of his wretchedness. And every time he lay down he said blindly, "Oh ye manitous!" though he did not know who the manitous were. Then he would eat. Sometimes he did not eat for 10 days. He continued to fast this way for 10 years. At that time, verily, he learned what he desired about life, and everything. Yea! It was even a fact that there were manitous. And for the first time he saw that he himself was possessed of the nature of a manitou. He saw the entire extent of the earth, and he saw clearly all the size of the sky as it hung. It was a fact that the manitous were many. This earth and sky were full of manitous. That is what he saw as soon as he had been blessed. Verily the manitous were everywhere. Indeed even he himself was possessed of the nature of a manitou. He for the first time saw how he was after he had blackened his face for 10 years and had starved himself. And for this length of time, surely 10 years, he went about wailing. He felt very certain and felt wretched. That is why he did so. And it is why he did not become discouraged during 10 years. And he first was blessed by a wolf and was first spoken to by him. It was a wolf who first paid attention to him as he wailed in wretchedness. "You will see everything of which you have thought, both what you thought today when I took pity upon you and what you thought when you did not know the manitou", he was told.

Verily yonder where he was first spoken to, there was a large lake called Menapī'tawa'i. The Meskwakies first came there when they came from across the great sea. Yonder also is where he was made to—(? e ta di si lwe e tti). That verily is why he felt so badly when he felt he was wretched. He was addressed at the northeast of (this lake).

(The wolf) began to lead him about where the manitous were, the representative manitous. (The wolf) said to them, "I bless this the future mortal", he said to his fellow manitous, "I bless him indeed in the exact manner he desired", he said to his fellow manitou, "because he did not know his chief who kept a fire for (i. e., had a town of) all who exist as mortals", he said to the one to whom they first came.

"And he also does not know how his life will extend. He desired that his life should continue as long as there was daylight. Therefore I blessed him that his life should be so. I blessed him with all that he desired", the wolf said to his fellow manitou, the manitou who sits fixedly in the east. And he also began to tell him that he blessed KepäyōmāwA. The latter accompanied the one who blessed him and led him around. And so eventually he (KepäyōmāwA) was spoken to (i. e., blessed) in the same way.

Whereupon he was also led to the south, and yonder the story of what he desired with regard to his life was told. And the manitou who dwells in the south was told, "We bless this mortal" (this manitou) was told by his fellow manitous, "we are not sufficient in number, for two of us blessed him", he was told. And he (the one blessed) was told then by the manitou who dwells in the south, "I shall not bless this one whom ye have blessed any differently" (the southern manitou) said. "I also shall bless him", he said. "I also shall not bless him differently. As ye have blessed him, I shall bless him", said the manitou who dwells in the south. "As he desires also a good life, his life shall be that way", he said, "as he desires to live to be old, I have granted it to be so. For he desired it to be so." In turn he addressed him. These (manitous) who had come to their fellow manitou in turn were addressed, "Now as many as we are, we shall not speak truthfully (i. e., our blessing will not be valid). We must go yonder to the west and tell there of his life."

And he began to be led to the west. And then they were four. They went and entered where (the manitou) who sits in the west dwelt. And the story of his life was told again. "Ho, we at last bring this person whom we blessed because he wailed wretchedly as he did not know how his life would continue to be in the future.

Therefore we blessed this our grandchild", he (the western manitou) was told by his fellow manitous, "that verily is why we bring him. And you must bless him in whatever way you desire. We ourselves have already spoken to (i. e., blessed) him. We have extended everything when we blessed him", he was told, And he (the western manitou) spoke telling how he blessed him, and said to them, "I shall not bless you any differently. As these indeed your grandfathers bless you I shall bless you. I shall not bless you differently than exactly what you desire regarding your life. For I was remembered, and when pity was taken upon you, you were brought to me. And this: I extend to him as much power as I possess. I do not withhold anything from him", he said. "I indeed extend to him as much power as I possess, all of it. I will bless with life each one of the mortals upon whose beings I took pity. Now this person upon whom ye had compassion surely blessed his body by continually wailing for 10 years. I shall not be able to bless him as I am but one. Verily today when you came, you were four. How shall I think not to bless him? Verily it is well that we bless him. We please him as he did not think uselessly. That is how our grandchild thought. But now as many as we are, we are not enough. Verily we must again go where (the manitou) dwells who is in the north, and tell about his life. We have not yet come to a decision over our grandchild. Therefore we shall go there and come to a decision regarding him."

Thereupon they departed. And indeed (the western manitou) accompanied them. So there were five. They went to the north and brought in the one whom they had blessed. And they came to the place where they were leading him. And again they spoke to their fellow manitou there and began to address him. They did not speak heedlessly to him. Surely in the order they blessed (Kepäy-ōmāwᴀ) was the order they spoke to him. The one who spoke first to (the northern manitou) was the one who first spoke to (i. e., blessed) Kepäyōmāwᴀ. Thereupon the one who blessed Kepäy-ōmāwᴀ the second time spoke to him. And indeed all spoke in order to their fellow manitou who dwells in the north. Verily this wolf was the one who spoke to him first; then (the manitou) who dwells in the east, the one who dwells in the south, and the one who dwells in the west. That verily is the order in which they spoke to him. Thereupon (the wolf) said to him: "We bring this person whom we bless. Verily as many as we now are is not enough. That is why we bring him." That is what the one who spoke first to him said to the (manitou) who dwells in the north. "Verily you must help us. Verily if you agree to this then whatever way we bless our grandchild will be valid. In vain we have told him how we bless him. We have extended to him all the power we have." Thereupon verily (the northern manitou) said, "How can it be that I also would not bless him? I also will bless our grandchild." Then he said to his fellow manitous, "I would like to listen to you (and learn) how you have blessed him."

SECTION 2

These indeed are the ceremonial attendants whenever the wolf hide is exposed: A member of the Wolf gens is indeed the head ceremonial attendant, and a member of the Bear gens. The Tō'kān is the leader and the Kī'ckō next. This is their way. Chickens, a hog, ducks, anything except dogs (are what they eat).

(1) Where they scald the chickens. After they have had their evening meal then they pluck them.[1]

(2) (The chickens) hang over the center of the fire at night. When the ceremonial attendants who work come early in the morning they are supposed to be always standing. These ceremonial attendants, both Tō'kāns and Kī'ckōs, invite anyone they wish.

(3) This is where the Kī'ckōs are seated.

(4) This is where the Tō'kāns are seated.

(5) And this is where the sacred pack is placed on top of a little matting. There is no mound of earth.

(6) Where the drummer sits down. (The person chosen) is not fixed.

(7) Those who rattle the gourds.

(8) A Kī'ckō woman.

(9) A Kī'ckō woman.

(10) A Tō'kān woman.

(11) A Tō'kān woman. There are no fixed rules as to gentes.

(12) Where the Kī'ckōs dance (?).

(13) Where the Tō'kāns dance.

(14) Where the kettles hang and where the fire is.

(15) Where the women who belong to this gens are seated.

(16) Also this is where women sit.

(17) Where the drum is put in order. The Kī'ckōs are on the south side and the Tō'kāns on the north.

(18) Where the director sits, the one who tells what they shall do.

(19) Where the head singer sits, who starts the songs.

(20) Where the bones which are left over are piled up.

(21) Where the flutes are placed.

They (two) ceremonial attendants untie the drum. The little keg is placed under the bench.

The sacred pack is displayed all this time. Only the wolf hide is in it.

In this ceremony no puppies are placed (by the sacred pack). But in other ceremonies they are (so) placed.

Maple sugar, strawberries, and watermelons (are suitable foods).

The upright poles are painted at the height of the breast of the painters. And they are painted green.

Only recently have (the men) worn coats (in these feasts). Long ago the Tō'kāns painted themselves black and the Kī'ckōs painted themselves white.

---

[1] See fig. 1.

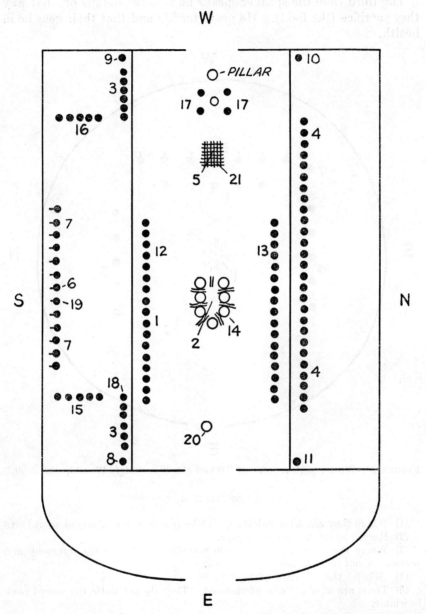

FIGURE 1.—Summer performance of "When the War Chiefs Worship the Wolf."

They are supposed to finish before sundown.

In the north was where this person was blessed.

The third time the speaker speaks he tells the details of what way they sacrifice (the food). He prays for life and that their gens be in health.

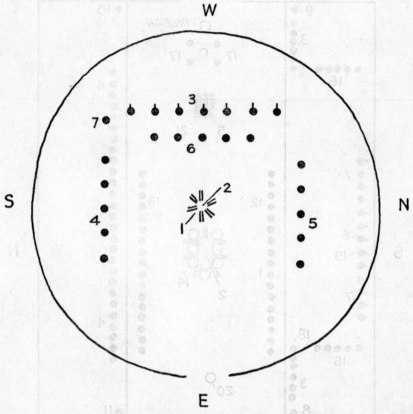

FIGURE 2.—Winter performance of "When the War Chiefs Worship the Wolf."

SECTION 3

(1) Where they scald the chickens. There is only one ceremonial attendant.[2]

(2) Here is where the offering hangs.

(3) Where the singers sit. They do not use a drum in this ceremony and women are not participants.

(4) (Where) those invited (sit).

(5) These are smokers who are invited. They do not untie the sacred pack in winter.

(6) Where the gourds are placed.

(7) Where the speaker sits.

---

[2] See fig. 2.

These eat once.   Anyone may eat.   Also red leaves may be offered. This is when it is winter.

Section 4

(This) is what is said in worship, and it is how the manitous, first the Spirit of Fire and then He Whose Eyes Bulge In The Smoke-Hole, are addressed in such worship.

"Your fellow manitous have placed you (two) here to correctly interpret to the manitous whatever our grandchildren continue to say (i. e., pray) to them, and to correctly report to them (our grandchildren's) tobacco, and also to whom their kettles (of food) are dedicated.   And now I shall address you, my grandfather, Spirit of Fire, and you Who Are In The Smoke-Hole, when we worship the manitous today, we who belong to one gens, as we pray that your fellow manitous whom we worship shall bless us.   Wherever we are you must bless your grandchildren with health and whatever span of life you have set for them.   That is what we ask of our grandfathers—life.   And moreover they must will away disease from us, and the chief as he kindles a fire for (i. e., has a town of) his men, his women, and his children.   And moreover if anyone from without shall talk against the chief's fire (i. e., town), he shall instead curse himself if he does not cease talking against our chief.   And moreover (we ask for) that which the one who bestowed the blessing placed last, namely, one slice. And also your fellow manitous have empowered you to bless every one of your grandchildren.   Verily you also must take compassion upon us, my grandfather, Spirit of Fire, and you Who Lie With Your Eyes Bulging In The Smoke-Hole.   In as many ways as we pray, you must think of us, and you will think of all of us who thus worship our grandfathers.   You must bless us with life.   (You will will away) disease.   The chief's fire [i. e., town] (shall rest peacefully).   Whoever from without speaks evilly against the chief's people (shall be unsuccessful).   And also (the manitous) did not bless (our venerable one) for a short time.   They blessed him until this earth lies old, when they took compassion upon him.   And the manitous set their blessing for the one upon whom they took compassion for as long as up to the time when the sky hangs old.   And (we ask for) one slice which (the manitous) gave as their last (boon to the one whom they blessed).   That, it seems, is as many ways as you blessed the one upon whom you took compassion.   And he wailed fearfully in wretchedness as he was wretched.   He wailed and went about blindly with open hands that he might learn where the manitous were.   'Have compassion upon me, my grandfathers,' he went about wailing (offering) his tobacco.   That is what we pray for.   My grandfather, Spirit of Fire, and You Who Dwell In The Smoke-Hole, you (both) must correctly interpret (the prayers of) your grandchildren to those who are worshiped.   You

(Who Dwell In The Smoke-Hole) know (each) inner thought. You know what your grandchildren think. Therefore you (both) will not fail to tell for them what they ask of their grandfathers, the manitous who bestow blessings as they worship them. You must not fail to tell (this) for them; that is what we say to you."

Section 5

"So he has done well today while it is daylight in worshiping his grandfather, the wolf hide, who bestowed the blessing. For he recognized that he did not know what would become of himself even the next day. That verily is why he acts as he does. Verily our chief pleases us all collectively in speaking for the entire extent of the fire (i. e., town) he guides, when worshiping. And we who belong to the War Chiefs gens are pleased for that exact reason. Men and ye women! You please us in coming here where our life is narrated, and in not refusing those whom we ordered (i. e., the ceremonial attendants). Verily you will benefit yourselves if the manitous whom we worship vouchsafe to us (our prayers). That is what we have told these two who watch over us here and know whatever we shall continue to think of ourselves (i. e., the Spirit of Fire and He Whose Face Bulges In The Smoke-Hole). And they, our grandfathers, the Spirit of Fire and He Who Dwells In The Smoke-Hole, will continue to inform their fellow manitous as they —(?) for us. We have given them tobacco to smoke first, so they will continue to ask precisely (what we want) because of the tobacco and cooked food. That is what we say to them upon whom we depend and who observe our lives as we live, for we who are of the last generation are wretched. They even listen to our songs. Also if we make mistakes in our songs, they must not refuse us and they must not reproach us. If we continue to make mistakes in our speeches, why, we should continue to speak. Exactly in as may ways as they granted blessings upon the one they blessed, we ask them to bless us. They must only bless us alike, for we wail in wretchedness as we worship and lament our lives, for we are wretched as we do not know what will happen to us in the future. We collectively pray for those of us who belong to this single gens, and then for all who belong to our chief's fire (i. e., town) as we wail continuously over our lives today while it is daylight. That verily is why we are pleased. As many of you as have come will benefit your lives even if you were here for a short time. At some place —(?) he was heard as he sent a message to each one of all those to whom he was related when he was reminded by the one who took compassion upon him: 'Those who took compassion upon me did not bless me for a short time. When this earth lies old is the limit they set for my (blessing) to continue to be valid. And when this sky hangs old is the limit our grandfather set for me when he took compassion upon me.' Indeed whoever shall sit solidly with us will in that way gain his life. And moreover, whoever shall carefully light the tobacco will thereby gain life. And also whoever shall carefully handle the worship when the manitous are extended the cooked food which is boiled will thereby gain life. And moreover, whoever will carefully eat what the manitous are offered in this worship will also obtain life that way. He will attain the span of old age exactly as it is set. And moreover, if anything continues to be hard (i. e., if there are hard times), he will get through if he carefully follows this (worship). For as many objects as are appurtentant to this worship is why we wail, men and ye women. That verily is why the one known by the manitous said, 'it is difficult.' That verily is why they say among themselves, 'We think it difficult.' Surely whoever shall think sincerely during the time worship is held will do so. Yet some do not think sincerely. They merely come where worship is held. Many do so. There may be four or there may be two (who are sincere). That is how we mortals are. That is to what extent we do not know that we shall be mindful of what the one worshiped said to the one upon whom he took compassion. And even before the worshiper has indeed (properly) finished (his worship) he prays: 'We are going out.' That is where we make an error. When he, the worshiper, is finished, then he removes us: 'Depart', he says to us. That verily is how the manitou has placed life. So I am trying to remind you how we depend upon (someone) to tell us what to do. We who are of the very last generation confirm what the manitous said when they said that we were wretched. Even they who were the first mortals paid attention to fasting and were blessed by the manitous. That is what they must have said. We are wretched, for we do not know at all how they presumably addressed the manitous. We follow the precepts (of our forefathers). That verily is why we wail as we worship. What we implore is that the manitous vouchsafe us what we desire. May they vouchsafe to us what we desire! Therefore ye had better eat. Eat! men and ye women. Now ye have done well in consuming all our offering. You may now leave us, men and women."

SECTION 6

(1) Where the ceremonial attendants place the chickens which they have plucked. What the one who initiated (the particular performance) brought is the first to be offered; what (the others bring) is (offered) in the order it was brought.[3]

(2) And this is where the ceremonial attendants eat first, early in the morning.

(3) And this is where the eaters throw away the left-over bones. As soon as the gens festival is over a ceremonial attendant is ordered to throw the bones

---

[3] See fig. 3.

wherever there is a thicket, where people do not go. "You throw them away", he is told. Then he is given tobacco and throws the bones away together with the tobacco, and he throws away tobacco together with the bones.

(4) Where the ceremonial attendants butcher and where they pile them up after they have finished plucking (the birds). And it is where they pile up (any) game animal early in the morning. And it is where they boil the harvest crop.

(5) And this is where (the food) is cooked which the ceremonial attendants will eat early in the morning.

(6) And this is where (the offering) of the leading celebrant of the gens festival is cooked.

(7) And this is where (offerings) are cooked in any order they are brought.

(8) This is where the flutes are which the ceremonial attendants will blow, and also where tobacco is. When (the ceremony) is completed only those who came to sit as givers of the gens festival are supposed to take it with them. That is why it is there.

(9) And this is where the sweet food is that has been brought.

(10) And this is where the sacred pack is which is worshiped.

(11) This is where the drum is placed which will be beaten.

(12) This is where the Tō'kāns always dance.

(13) And this is where the Kī'ckōs dance.

(14) This is where the women who hum, that is, who are female Tō'kāns, sit.

(15) And this is where the Kī'ckō women who hum sit.

(16) This is where the smokers and dancers sit, Kī'ckōs and Tō'kāns being all mixed up.

(17) And this is where the singers sit.

(18) Here is where those sit who have come to sit as givers of the gens festival and who have come to listen, only those who do not know how to sing; girls also.

(19) And this is where one ceremonial attendant dances. He is a leading ceremonial attendant and is supposed to be a Kī'ckō.

(20) And this also is a leading ceremonial attendant, and this ceremonial attendant is said to be a Tō'kān.

(21) And these are merely those who have to watch on and who have come to eat; dancers also are with them.

SECTION 7

The ceremonial attendants would pick chickens the night before the festival. The fire is made by flint. Water is first heated, then the feathers are plucked. The ceremonial attendants eat after their work is done. The morning of the festival the chickens are dressed and cut in pieces. There are four kettles. The first is in the southeast, the second in the west, the third in the northwest, the fourth in the northeast; all are toward the east end of the summer house. Usually women fix up the mattings at the east end. The drum is fixed early in the morning of the feast, immediately after the chickens have been cut up. The waiters may be Kī'ckōs or Tō'kāns; it makes no difference. It does as regards the dancers. There are four women who hum, two are Kī'ckōs and two are Tō'kāns, irrespective of gentes; women who can hum are chosen. When dancing the Tō'kāns will be on the north side and the Kī'ckōs on the south side. There is no dancing in a circle. When the cere-

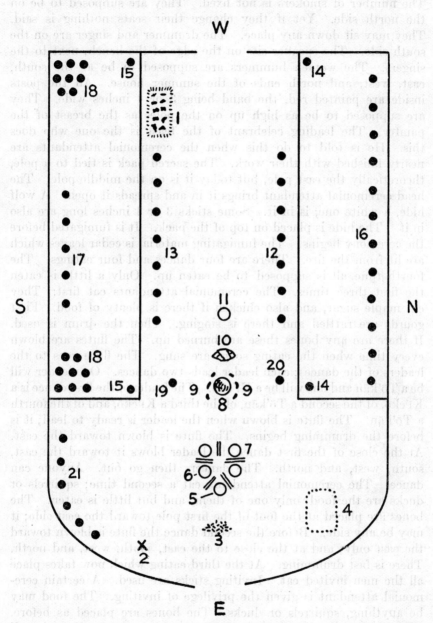

FIGURE 3.—Summer performance of "When the War Chiefs Worship the Wolf" (different informant).

monial attendants are ready those celebrating the festival enter. The number of smokers is not fixed. They are supposed to be on the north side. Yet if they change their seats nothing is said. They may sit down any place. The drummer and singer are on the south side. The speaker sits on the edge of the bench, next to the singers. The women hummers are supposed to be at the south, east, west, and north ends of the summer house. All the posts inside are painted red, the band being 3 or 4 inches wide. They are supposed to be as high up on the poles as the breast of the painter. The leading celebrant of the feast is the one who does this. He is told to do this when the ceremonial attendants are nearly finished with their work. The sacred pack is tied to a pole, theoretically the east pole, but today it is on the middle pole. The head ceremonial attendant brings it in and spreads it open. A wolf hide, a white one, is in it. Some sticks 3 or 4 inches long are also in it. The hide is placed on top of the pack. It is fumigated before the ceremony begins. The fumigating material is cedar leaves which are lit from the fire. There are four dances and four eatings. The fourth time all is supposed to be eaten up. Only a little is eaten the first three times. The ceremonial attendants eat first: They eat maple sugar, and also chicken if there is plenty of food. First gourds are rattled and there is singing. Then the drum is used. If there are any bones these are burned up. The flutes are blown every time when the eating songs are sung. The flute goes to the leaders of the dances; each leader leads two dances. One leader will be a Tō'kān and one will be a Kī'ckō. The leader of the first dance is a Kī'ckō, of the second a Tō'kān, of the third a Kī'ckō, and of the fourth a Tō'kān. The flute is blown when the leader is ready to lead; it is before the drumming begins. The flute is blown toward the east. At the close of the first dance the leader blows it toward the east, south, west, and north. The dancers then go out. Anyone can dance. The ceremonial attendants eat a second time; squirrels or ducks are the food; only one of them; and but little is eaten. The bones are placed at the foot of the first pole toward the east side; it may be any side. Before the second dance the flute is blown toward the east only; and at the close to the east, south, west, and north. There is fast drumming. At the third eating which now takes place all the men invited eat. Inviting sticks are used. A certain ceremonial attendant is given the privilege of inviting. The food may be anything, squirrels or ducks. The bones are placed as before. The flutes are used as in the second dance. At the fourth eating all the people eat, children included, as long as the food lasts. The bones are disposed of as above. Inviting sticks are not used. The fourth dance now follows. The flute is used as before. At the close of the dance all go out, but an old man speaks, tells the story of the man who was blessed in the early days. The people are supposed to stay and listen to this, but today many go out. The prayers by the old men (not determined) during the eating are for life, freedom from disease, that if anyone outside the village speaks or makes an imprecation against the chief, he shall be unsuccessful. Some ask for one slice, some ask that they be not ashamed at the final day. The name of the person blessed who instituted this ceremony is KepäyōmāwA. In the beginning there was no religion on the earth. The time came when the people realized there ought to be some. So they fasted, wondering if there were any gods (manitous). They fasted and wailed, and received blessings; this is how this fellow obtained this blessing.

SECTION 8

(1) A pole which stands near the door toward the east.[4]

(2) And this is another pole.

(3) Indeed another pole.

(4) And another. These all stand toward the south.

(5) And this pole stands toward the north.

(6) Another one.

(7) And another one.

(8) And another one.

(9) And this pillar in the center is a big one.

(10) And still another.

(11) This is where the sacred pack is.

(12) This is the fire.

(13) The doorway toward the east.

(14) The doorway toward the west.

(15) A kettle in which is the squirrel which the ceremonial attendants will eat early in the morning.

(16) (A kettle in which) must be a hog.

(17) (A kettle in which) must be duck(s), the main food when the wolf hide is worshiped.

(18) (A kettle in which is the food) which the medicine people (me te wa ki) eat.

(19, 20, 21) (Kettles which contain) any (food) which the manitous eat; but no dogs are used in this ceremony.

(22) This is where a Kī'ckō woman who sits and represents sits.

(23) Where (another) Kī'ckō (woman who sits and represents is), toward the west.

(24) A Tō'kān woman who sits and represents.

(25) Another Tō'kān woman. (Beyond these) they are not set; simply (any women) who can hum.

(26) The ceremonial attendant who fetches this earth brings tobacco. (The earth is earth) which has not been stepped on. (Females) who do not menstruate continue to bring (tobacco). That is how this is fetched. And this earth which is piled up in a lump (and made into) a mound is not brought. It is merely placed where the little sacred pack is to lie. (The mound) is merely underneath. That is what they do.

---

[4] See fig. 4.

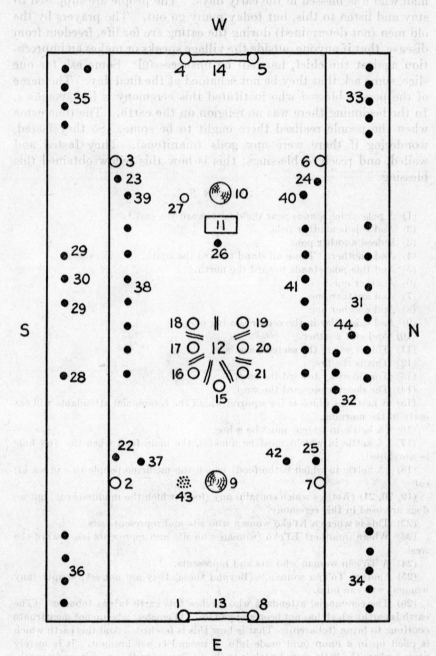

FIGURE 4.—Same performance as figure 3 (different informant).

(27) This is where this drum (kettle) is after it has been tied up. These are they who usually make it: A member of the Wolf gens, a member of the Bear gens, a member of the Feathered (Thunder) gens, a member of the Dirty Little Ani.

(28) This is the speaker, Shawata.

(29) These are singers.

(30) The drummer is Ki dka ta li wa (Harrison Kapayou); the singers are Wi di ka kya (John Jones), No ka wa ta (Bill Leaf), and Ta ta la ko (John Leaf).

(31) These are the smokers.

(32) Where the ceremonial attendants sit.

(33) Women and children.

(34) Women and children.

(35) Only the women who sit as celebrants of the festival. Wa sa na ᴀ (Mary Peters), who is not a celebrant, sits with them.

(36) This also is where women and children sit.

(37) A woman who is a Kī'ckō and a dancer.

(38) Men who are Kī'ckōs and dancers.

(39) A woman who is a Kī'ckō.

(40) A woman who dances and is a Tō'kān.

(41) Men who dance and are Tō'kāns.

(42) A Tō'kān woman. They are not particular whether the women who dance are Kī'ckōs or Tō'kāns.

(43) This is where they pile up the bones which are left over (by the wolves?).

(44) This is the speaker who prays when they have eaten for the last time, Ma gi la na da ᴀ, Young Bear.

Sha wa ta, an old man.
Di di ga ne sa (John Bear).
Li da ᴀ (Harrison Kapayou), drummer.
No ka wa ta (Bill Leaf), singer.
Wi di ka kya (John Jones), singer.
Ta ta la ko ᴀ (John Leaf), leader of the songs.
Dawate (Shawata) is he who blows the flute.

These are the women:

Wa so se ᴀ (Sam Slick's aged mother, recently deceased).
A sa wa sa mo (Mrs. John Pete).
Ne ta ko se (Little Harry Johnson's mother).
Na wa te (Mrs. J. Wayne).
Ne wa ki ki (Caesar's wife; mother of John Roberts).

Section 9

THE WOLF DANCE OF THE WAR CHIEFS GENS: WHAT HAPPENED AT JOHN BEAR'S, JUNE 4, 1924

Well, a ceremonial attendant said, "Everything is now boiling." Then a leading singer started to rise to his feet. This is what he did. He walked around the fire four times. After he had walked in a circle [and stopped on the south side of the fire] he cast tobacco on the fire and began making a speech: "Now, my grandfather, I give you a smoke of this tobacco. This verily is what we desire of you: Life, and nothing else, so be it. For you, so be it, have been given the privilege, so be it, of watching over your grandchildren, so be it. That verily, so be it, is why I today, so be it, burn (this tobacco) for you, my grandfather, and why we offer in advance some squirrels. That verily, so be it, is how I have made my offering to you. We sacrifice this to this (leading) Wolf. He verily is one who knows that he dwells well as he leans on good earth (?). It is now spring. Therefore, so be it, we are very glad that we eat well in this summer, and that we have not disease is very fine. That verily is what we say to this Wolf who dwells in the wilderness. That indeed is what I say. It is what I say to you. And what I say to him Whose Eyes Bulge In The Smoke-Hole is that he carefully transmit our prayer to (the manitou). That is what I say to you this day."

Then they sang. The first song was:

Wi i ya wi i ya wi ya;
This sky here, e e e;
Wi i ya wi i ya wi ya;
This sky here, e e e.

[Wi i ya wi i ya wi ya;
Ma ni yo ki de gi, e e e;
Wi i ya wi i ya wi ya;
Ma ni yo ki de gi, e e e.]

And after they had sung the one (who spoke before) made a speech: "Well, all ye to whom I am related: It is fine that you are seated in a cluster (i. e., are with us) today. Ye also are seated in a cluster (desiring) life. We see with gladness that you have come." They (the people) then said, "Yea!"

The second song was:

Well, today; well, today;
We speak, we speak, a a a.

[Na i i no ki; na i i no ki;
Ne ke to le na, ne ke to le na, A A A.]

And he was told this, "Very well!"

Now when a ceremonial attendant had done cooking he served meat in a dish there. Then this single ceremonial attendant (mentioned above) was given this meat. That is what they did.

Then as the ceremonial attendant served the (food) he passed the dish in a circle four times around the kettle, and the second (dish) three times, and the third (dish) twice, and the very last (dish) once. From then on it was just once. That is the way they always do with these others.

When (the ceremonial attendant) had finished serving (the food) a single speaker spoke again. He told why he was worshiping. As

soon as he had spoken they began to eat.   And they began to sing.
This is how it went:

I begin to eat, I begin to eat;
(Repeat twice.)
I am a manitou,
I am a manitou;
You are a manitou,
You are a manitou;
This indeed is your land,
This indeed is your land.

[Ne wi li se nye   ne wi li se nye;
(Repeat twice.)
E ma ne to wi ya ni,
E ma ne to wi ya ni;
Ki na   yo   ke ma ne to wi,
Ki no   yo   ke ma no to wi;
Ki na   yo   ke ta ki mi   ma ni   yo o,
Ki na   yo   ke ta ki mi   ma ni   yo o.]

Then they began to eat.

  (1) A smoker.[5]
  (2) A smoker.
  (3) A smoker.
  (4) A smoker.
  (5) A smoker.
  (6) A smoker.
  (7) A smoker.
  (8) A smoker.
  (9) The kettles.
(10) Where the ceremonial attendants are.
(11) The sacred pack.
(12) The singers.

This is how they sat.   They ate where they sat.   That is how it
was.   After they had eaten all (that was served) then they were
served ducks, pumpkins, squashes, Indian corn meal.   After they
had eaten all then the speaker again began speaking: "Now you have
done well in coming to where we worship.   We are not worshiping
for (our own advantage) alone.   We are also worshiping for you.
So the manitou will think of you and bless you so that you will live
in good health."   That is what they said among themselves.   "Therefore you may now leave us", the speaker said.   That is all he said.

"This is the way they did.   They were after the Sioux.   These
Indians fasted several days.   And so, it seems, this one man fasted
several days when he was after the Sioux.   But he fasted too many
days.   And so, it seems, he was blessed.   Verily this worship goes
back to that.   And they also spread this fumigating material on the
top of a bark house for one summer (to dry).   Then it becomes

---

[5] See fig. 5.

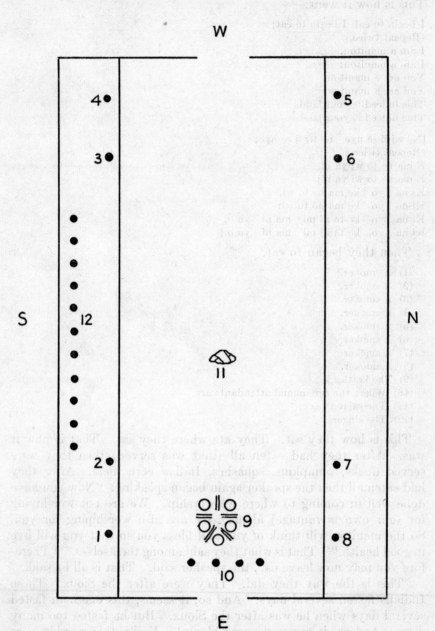

FIGURE 5.—Same performance as figure 3 (different informant).

suitable. So they say. That is what they say when they tell this. And dancers also dance with these scalps when they dance. Those who celebrate the gens festival have six of them. Three are Sioux scalps and three are Pawnee scalps. They are likewise fumigated. But they are thoroughly fumigated. That is how it is. This is why they do it. I have thoroughly informed you", the speaker said to them when he informed them. "Whenever we have danced vigorously, then the information should be given in detail", he said to them. "That is how this is. If anyone (thinks) 'I desire to know it', he should dedicate something." That is what he said to these who were seated in a row. Then he ceased speaking. "Well, again", he said to them, "if we do this again, anyone who comes will know it thoroughly." That was what he said. There is, to be sure, much more for me to tell, but I have entirely lost it, and cannot tell it. Soon I may be able to tell it. That is as far as I inform you.

SECTION 10

Now that you have come this day to ask me for information, you shall receive every particular part, and I am sure I can give it all to you. I may tell you as much as I know, but remember not to say anything to anyone. It is against our rules to give this information. That is the reason why I shall not give you all. But I will give it to you after I see our leader, and I shall try to give you that information.

You have asked how this was obtained. Every religion was gotten from visions. Those who received the visions fasted for several days. And the reason they received the blessings was because they had fasted so many days. And this particular man of whom we are speaking did something wonderful for his fellow people. And we are strictly prohibited from giving his name. So I cannot mention his name to you today.[6] Later on I will give you a little information. Soon I will tell you. The information will be quite lengthy, and I don't think we have time enough to get this information, as we who are members of this gens are still telling each other, and even we have not received all the information. But you have asked so many questions and I will not give this information at this time. And another thing, (orthodoxly) it is very slow in getting everything in it. But the way we are to do is a very fast time. For that reason we won't get every bit of it. And I will skip many things on which you have questioned me. And that is because I wish to have plenty of time. But I will do the best I can to explain it to you.

Remember that I told you at the beginning that each person (who received blessings) fasted and that was why he was blessed. That is what this person (who inaugurated the Wolf Dance of the War Chiefs gens) did: He fasted earnestly. It was now quite winterish.

---

[6] As stated by other informants, his name was Kepäyōmāwᴀ.

It was near the shore of the great sea. It seems it was near the shore of the great sea where what is now called "Chicago" is; it was west of it and at the edge of the water. That is what has been told us. And he fasted very earnestly, so we are told. Surely he probably fasted for several days. We do not know how many days exactly. That is how he received his blessing.

Right after this the people fought with the English and French as soon as the English and French had come. Then the Meskwakies ceased to be willing to fast.

Then, it seems, this man, the one who was blessed, was told what to do. And he gave instructions. That is what he did. He kept on telling these Indians what they should do and that they were to tell the succeeding generations. Verily they did so. They told each other from generation to generation about this worship. No one (today) has seen those who were blessed (and know) what they did long ago. We who are mortals tell each other how this worship is. That is why we know it. Only indeed a person who is intelligent is one who can comprehend it. It is very difficult to be comprehended. I am telling you how it is.

And the one who was blessed was clean, and he did not bother with women at all. These men who fasted did not bother with women. A long time ago that was how they fasted. Young men were forbidden to fool with women: That is how it was possible for them to be blessed by the manitous. And today we do not amount to anything. We are merely bad. That is why we know nothing.

Now this is a summer house. This is how it is when they dance. I shall tell you today how it is:

(1) Singers.[7]
(2) A Kī'ckō hummer.
(3) A Tō'kān hummer.
(4) A Tō'kān hummer.
(5) A Kī'ckō hummer.
(6) Fire.
(7) Where the sacred pack is.
(8) This is the dancers.
(9) Smokers who are invited.
(10) Ceremonial attendants.
(11) This is where the drum is.

And they do not dance in a circle: They merely dance in a fixed position. This is what they do.

These ceremonial attendants are supposed to be members of the Wolf gens. That is how it is.

I am giving you full information.

Oh, they offer those with downy feathers (i. e., birds) when they celebrate a gens festival. And this: When a fire is made none of

---

[7] See fig. 6.

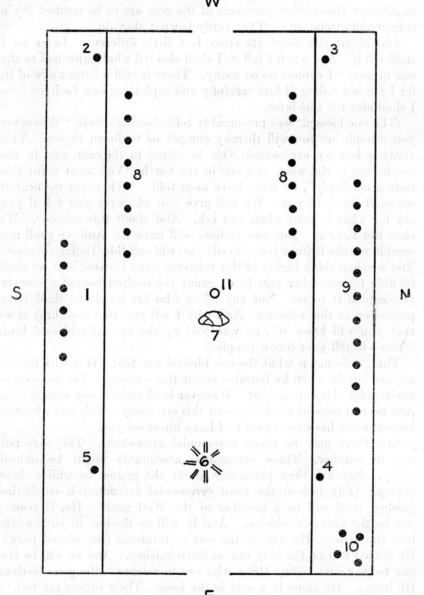

FIGURE 6.—Same performance as figure 3 (different informant).

this fire is used (i. e., no matches are used). Most assuredly Indian fire is used when there is worship. That is what the old men have told us. And whenever a gens festival is to be held, about 10 days in advance these fellow members of the gens are to be notified (by a ceremonial attendant). That verily is what they do.

And about this flag: Its story is a little different. Later on I shall tell it. And when I tell it, I shall also tell what happened to the one blessed. I cannot do so today. There is still a little more of it, for I am not telling of him carefully and explaining how he lived. So I shall also tell this later.

(The one blessed) was presumably told about the flute, "Whenever you worship us you will thereby compel us to listen to you. This verily is how we are seated: One is seated in the east, one in the south, one in the west, and one in the north. You must point this flute accordingly", he must have been told. "Whenever we hear it we shall listen to you. We will give you whatever you ask if you ask for what is good when you ask. And about this tobacco. We shall not have it. But you Indians will have it. And we shall not be able to take it from you. Verily you will call this 'Indian tobacco.' And we shall think highly of this tobacco. And because of it we shall be able to remember you (i. e., grant the desired boons) whenever you extend it to us. Not any of us who are manitous shall have possession of this tobacco. And why I tell you this one thing is so that you will know it", he was told by the one who blessed him. "You will tell your fellow people."

That, it seems, is what the one blessed was told. It is why indeed anyone is told when he inquires about this worship. Yet not everyone is told. He is looked at. Whoever is all right is one who is told. And no evil persons are told about this ceremony. This one who was blessed must have been told as I have informed you.

And there may be many ceremonial attendants. They are not few in number. These ceremonial attendants might be indeed many. Nor are they particular about the gentes to which these belong. Only indeed the head ceremonial attendant is so distinguished (and will be a member of the Wolf gens). He, it seems, will be the first one selected. And he will be the one to pour water into the drum. He will be the one to fumigate (the sacred pack). He indeed will be the only one so distinguished. And he will be the one to go about telling those who are to celebrate the gens festival (to hunt). He alone in a way is the boss. These others are not.

Moreover, those who are members of this gens only hold their festival after it is full spring. They do not hold their festival early in spring. After the leaves are large is when they celebrate their gens festival. After it is harvest then they also celebrate their festival. And this is how they sit. I will also tell later on how the

eaters sit after I have told you all. I have not yet started to tell
you anything important. I have told you how a little of it is.

Also when the members of this gens hold death wakes their ceremonies are a little different (from those of other gentes). That is
how they are. And the women still nowadays fast before the gens
festival is celebrated. They still always do so. And the men once
in a while still fast (before the ceremony). But they do not speak of
it. That is how they are. And they are under religious interdiction
not to kill these snakes which crawl about. That is how they are.
They nowadays still forbid each other to kill those who fly around
and have downy feathers (just for fun, or for ordinary food). Even
the children are cautioned not to kill birds. That is one thing those
of this gens have told each other from generation to generation.
They still do so. And this is what they say when they make their
speeches in the festivals. Life is the one thing which they mention

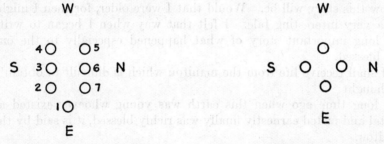

ARRANGEMENT OF KETTLES   ARRANGEMENT OF KETTLES
IN HARVEST FESTIVAL   IN WINTER FESTIVAL

FIGURE 7.—Arrangement of the kettles (same informant).

with great emphasis. And "one slice" is one thing. That disease
may not come among them is also one thing. Likewise that no one
think evilly against this town where they have their village. That
is what they say in their speeches when they worship. And if anyone
goes about speaking evilly against them, that they be unsuccessful
in their designs. That is what they say in their speeches. Also
that everything be well. That is what they continue to say. Moreover that they live to old age. That is also one thing for which they
pray.

Well, I have now told you what these who worship ask for. And
I shall tell you later on the name of the one blessed. (I have indeed
told you) a little, but that is as far as I shall tell you today. Oh,
I did not tell you how the kettles are hung. This is how the ceremonial attendants hang the kettles whenever they hold their festivals
in the harvest time: (fig. 7). And this is how they should hang
them at a gens festival (when there is no dancing, i. e., in winter),
when there is simply a festival (fig. 7). I might indeed tell more

after they have had their festival. I might tell you very soon. That
is all.

Now there is one man who is the leading dancer. He is a Tō'kān.
And there is one Kī'ckō (dancer). First the Tō'kān is the leader,
then the Kī'ckō, then the Tō'kān, then the Kī'ckō, then the Tō'kān.
That is what they do. And they are not in the habit of speaking to
women who are menstruating: It is against their religion. That is
all I tell you today.

SECTION 11

This is about one man a long time before the white men came here.
As I relate this today, it is not really I (who am responsible): It is
narrated as I heard (the narrators). And if they made mistakes in
what they said I shall indeed make mistakes in what I say when nar-
rating this today. But I shall tell the story very carefully as the old
men told me. I shall surely narrate it exactly as I heard it. That
is how this story will be. Would that I were older, for then I might
tell a very interesting tale. I felt that way when I began to write
this long important story of what happened especially to the one
first blessed.

"I shall receive life from the manitou which is difficult to obtain",
he thought.

A long time ago when this earth was young whoever existed as
mortal and fasted earnestly finally was richly blessed, it is said by the
manitou.

But nothing, it seems, happened to him. And as I tell it now, he
indeed existed as a mortal a second time, but he did not know that he
had existed as a mortal.

What I tell today is very difficult, and there is indeed much of it.

Now indeed I shall tell of this man. Soon, it seems, he was born
among the Meskwakies. Well, he kept on living here. He did not
even have a name as he was very poor. He looked again and again
at the Spirit of Fire, it seems, so it is said. Finally as he was gazing
at the Spirit of Fire, it blazed, so it is said. "Well!" he thought,
"this one is greatly endowed with mystic power", he thought, so it
seems. And soon he also thought, "We who are mortals are indeed
very wretched", he thought, it is said. "Tomorrow I shall go and
wail"! he thought, "for I know all too little about how my life is.
I do not even know how my life will be in the future", he thought, it is
said.

So early the next morning he started to take down his tobacco and
burned it for the Spirit of Fire. "Now, my grandfather, today I give
you this tobacco to smoke as I wail for my life", he said to him. As
he went out he shrieked blindly as he wandered far off in the wilderness. He went about wailing. And when he saw anything that

appeared mysterious he took his tobacco and cast it on it. "My grandfathers! Manitous! Because I am indeed wretched is why I go about wailing", he said to it, it is said. Finally he did as I have said to each thing he saw in succession. "Have pity upon me whoever you are, for you know the extent (the manitou) has set my life to be", he said to it.

Finally he walked back to where he came from and ate.

And the next morning he went far off, blindly with open hands, that he might know where the manitou dwelt. He simply thought anything was a manitou and scattered his tobacco. Well, in exactly 10 days he came back to eat. That verily is what I narrate. He did not know anything. Therefore he again departed. And he came back. He had been going about wailing the third time. And again he merely ate and departed, it is said. That indeed is what happened to him. So, it is said, he was addressed by a manitou. It was a wolf. It was a black one, so it is said. "Now today, my grandchild, I bless you," it said that he was told. He was blessed by a manitou, a black wolf. "But by myself I am not able to bless you so that (my blessing) will be valid", (the wolf) said to him, it is said. "But let us go yonder", he was told. And he was taken to the east, it is said. "Now this day I bring this my grandchild. I took pity upon him as he wailed bitterly because he did not know how his life was. He thought his life was very wretched. That is why I took pity upon him", this wolf said to this manitou who dwells in the east. "I blessed him particularly because of the four quarters, and he will be successful in war four times. Now why I took pity upon him today is because he wailed too terribly."

"It is a very good thing that you have done in blessing the one upon whom you took pity. What I say to you this day is that I also bless him in exactly the same way in which you took compassion upon him. Surely I also take compassion upon him in the same way", they were told by the manitou. "You must indeed in addition take him yonder. For as we are now merely two who bless him, it is not enough", said this manitou.

So they went out again, departed and went to where a manitou dwelt in the south, it is said. They went to see him, it is said. That verily is what is related. And when they suddenly came yonder where a fellow manitou was (the black wolf said), "We have told you how wretched our grandchild was." Oh, I shall not take compassion upon whom you have blessed in any other way", he thought, it is said. Finally he was reminded. "This one is named 'Ke le yo ma wa' ", he was told.

And he (Ke le yo ma wa=Kepäyōmāwᴀ) was told exactly the same thing. He was blessed in every kind of way, even so that he himself might bless the people. "In whatever way you bless anyone, the same shall happen to him", he was told when he was given the blessing.

Now at almost this time the people were willed to be ruined by his people. At that time the son of a great manitou, WâpAʻsaiyA (White Robe), already was dwelling here. He had already been born, it is said.

Well, he (Ke le yo ma wa) was led to the west where another manitou was. "We have come to see you", he was told, it is said. Now verily the reason why he has been led about insistently is because only if (all the manitous) were willing would (their blessings) come true: If, however, any one were unwilling then the manner in which (the first manitou) blessed (Ke le yo ma wa) their grandchild would be a failure. Well, they came to the west and were told, "You are walking around. When this our grandchild went about wailing in anguish only I took pity upon him. That is why I come. 'For as I am but one, it is not enough if I alone bless him.' So I thought. That is why I now lead him about", he was told. "Now you have done well this day in blessing our grandchild. As you have spoken, so shall I also bless him. But we are not enough. You must lead him to the north. (The manitou there) will dismiss him", they were told.

So, it is said, they again departed and when they came to the north they were told, "You are walking about." "Oh, I blessed our grandchild" (the first manitou) said. "You have done well", he was told by the one in the distant north. "You must lead him in person to where the Great Manitou dwells above. You must lead him there. He will be able to dismiss you. In whatever way you have spoken to him, so shall I. That verily is what I tell you", he was told, it is said.

Thereupon he (the wolf) led him where the Great Manitou dwells up above and spoke to him: "This verily is what I say to you this day as I come, as we come here in the country of the Great Manitou."

"I am very glad that you all have blessed our grandchild. For that is what I said to you formerly. 'I made a great mistake', I said to you formerly. At that time I gave you permission to take pity upon the people for my sake. Now we even blessed this man formerly four times; today he is reincarnate. Verily this mortal's name formerly was 'Ke le yo ma wa'; and today his name is exactly the same. The way you (sing.) blessed him will be again the same", they were told. "Now as you blessed him I grant you (the wolf) to live with him for as long as our fellow manitous shall not change this our earth. That is the extent of time you will be with him. That verily is what I say to you today", is what, it is said, (the wolf) was told. That, it is said, is what they were to do.

"Well, my friend", (the wolf) said to (Ke le yo ma wa), "whenever you have completed your plans, come and fetch me", so he was told. "If you merely see the hide (of a wolf) anywhere it will be my body. You will watch (?) it as long as you worship me. Now I must go to the east. You may come to fetch me", he said to him, so it is said.

That is what he did. Then, it is said, he employed a ceremonial attendant. He boiled game. Dogs were never offered when (the wolf) was worshiped, merely any little thing, game animals, fowls, any living things.

Then, it is said, those named gathered and brought various little living things. So when they had everything boiling he departed and walked to the east, and when he came yonder, lo, on a tree (the wolf hide) was hanging; so he took it down. "Carefully", he was told. "Do not handle it roughly", he was told, it is said. Thereupon, it is said, he brought it, it seems, where they lived and brought it inside. "Well, this is our grandfather", he said to the people. He who is here will especially be the first (to be worshiped). There is no other worship here. Only when they celebrate the Mystic Rite shall they have it here.

"Now, ceremonial attendants", they were told. "As you are ceremonial attendants today you will fetch earth. You will place clean earth here in the center. You will hang this (wolf hide) there", they were told. "I do not have many songs. They will be made later on. When they are made there will be many of them. When they go to war each will return with a song. That is why the songs are few." That verily is what he told them.

Then, it is said, they brought this earth and placed clean earth in the center. Then the wolf hide was hung there.[8] It was hung open, it is said. That is what they say.

At this time they did not do very much. At that time, it is said, there were many men dancers. That, it is said, is what they did when they first danced. As soon as they had danced (Ke le yo ma wa) gave speeches, it is said, explaining what happened separately to him. Truly he did not talk blindly. It was exactly as he had been addressed by the manitou. For 40 days he had not eaten. Then for the first time was it possible for him to secure a blessing. "Now men as I address you today I only tell you what is good. Therefore I now finish my talk."

Then, it is said, he prayed, and when he was listened to the first time, he said, "Well, all ye to whom I am related! This day the manitous have blessed me. I shall explain it to you", he said to them. "Listen carefully to me", he said. "This day I starve myself", he said, according to tradition. "Because I do not know how far my life will extend. That is why I do as I do this day. I am very glad

[8] See fig. 8.

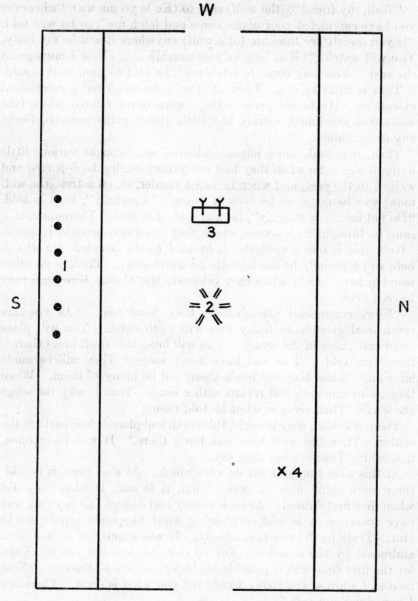

1 - THOSE WHO WORSHIP WHERE THEY SIT
2 - FIRE
3 - WHERE THE WOLF HIDE HANGS
4 - WHERE THEY DRESSED OFFERINGS

FIGURE 8.—Where the wolf hide hangs (same informant as for figure 4).

that you have come here, for the manitou sees you and blesses you with life. If I had not done this, you would be very wretched. Do your best, friends, to be constantly seated at the worship of this manitou who took pity upon me. Surely he took pity upon me. But as for you, only if you are constantly seated at the worship of the manitou who blessed me will you obtain life." So the man spoke, it is said. "I shall still give you instructions. Finally this my grandfather came and blessed me. That is why I carefully explain it to you. Come, this day I am going to war. I shall be the leader of the war party. I shall fetch some human beings", he said, according to tradition. As soon as he had given them instructions then he began to say, "Now it seems that this my grandfather led me widely about yonder. He led me to the east where a manitou dwells. He addressed me the same way. As soon as he had spoken to me, then (the wolf) led me to the south, and he spoke of me there. And when we again came there the manitou spoke to me exactly as the other had said. That verily is what I say. And he led us west. Soon we were on our way there. And then (the wolf) explained (to the manitou there) how he had taken pity upon me. (The manitou there) was greatly pleased. Soon he began saying the very same, for he was glad. So he said. And he sent us to the north where (a manitou) dwells. Soon we came there. And as soon as we arrived (the wolf) said to him, 'I have indeed blessed this our grandchild.' So he said. And soon (the manitou) there blessed me again. That is what he did. Thereupon the one who dwells in the north sent us up above. That is what happened to us. And when we arrived yonder where the Great Manitou dwells, he also took pity upon me. He was very glad at what my grandfather had done. 'I am very glad at what you have done', my grandfather was told. 'I rejoice that you (manitous) bless each one of my grandchildren. So I rejoice.' So said the Great Manitou. 'And you (addressing the wolf) will go and dwell with him.' So he is here. I am very glad that all of you are here today as I worship", he said.

These War Chiefs were told "Yea!" by the people.

Then he had already been named to be chief. But he could not do so. He already had been named to be of the War Chiefs gens.

Therefore I tell according to traditions how these worshipers were well taken care of.

Yet they were ever at war. All day long they feasted and worshiped the manitou. They saw the wolf plainly. At that time there was very sincere worship. And they never ceased to worship (the wolf) for even a moment. That is what they did at that time, according to tradition. And they went to war, it is said, and departed the next day. Where they were aiming for was close by. There were many in the war party, so it is said. Finally they came yonder to a Sioux village. And at that time White Robe (WāpaʻsaiyA) was staying with them. His friend was Na sa li lya ta. And this Ke le yo ma wa was the leader of the war party. There was a great slaughter. (His) men indeed slaughtered many of the people. They struck down one village, it is said, including children and women. (Ke le yo ma wa's men) were very brave. Then, it is said they departed back (to their homes). The men related exactly what I have narrated this day.

And soon they were made to suffer. These two men had already been made warriors. And this one, WâpaʻsaiyA (White Robe), had not fasted. When he was told to fast he would say "Why?" "You will become a brave warrior, and moreover you will not be shot (by a war missile)", he was told, so it is said. "Perhaps you think of me, 'he does not dream.' I certainly shall dream all night. Why don't you dream?" the man was asked whose son was this White Robe (WâpaʻsaiyA). "Why don't you fast?" he asked his father. "I earnestly desire to dream", he said to him, it is said, "I ever dream too much", he said to his father. "Perhaps if I did not sleep all night I should not dream so often", he said to him, according to tradition. That is what is related of him.

Now it is said that he was very powerful. "This fellow is still taken care of here", (?) is what they said. And when they came back they made each other dance vigorously. They had very enjoyable times.

Well, as I tell the story today, they finally, they soon came back and worshiped. "Well, let us gather. We have had a very hard time", the people would say to each other as they were brave (?). Then they would go to worship. "Now indeed you have the power of each becoming a warrior" (the leader) said to the people. "As for me, I enjoy it very much", he would say to them; "you are strange" he would say to them. "I enjoyed it greatly yonder", he said.

"They had not come for war", he was told, "they were not our foes." If they had not thought that at once (they would have made a better showing). "They must have been tired or they would have slain you all. If you had to go at them they would have slain you all."

Soon they held a council, desiring him to become chief. That is what they said to him. And as soon as the men had made a decision they went and summoned him. "You are summoned to the chief's dwelling", he was told. "Very well", he said. He started to enter. "Why is it that you summon me?" they were asked. "Well, my friend, these men appoint you to be chief", he was told. "Verily you will assent to what is determined for you. You will be chief", he was told. And he sat with his head lowered. "Well, what must I do?" he said to them. "Well, you will cease going to war. You will sit quietly in one spot", this chieftain said to him. "You (pl.) will be chiefs." And this one who was called Ke le yo ma wa was told, "We who formerly were War Chiefs shall now be chiefs." They said so, it is said, and went and sat down comfortably. The next day he said, "I shall be chief", and sat down comfortably. "Such men", they said among themselves. If any (captive) came they said among themselves, "Let him depart peacefully", so it is said. Soon, when 10 days were up, this fellow rose from his seat and said, "It is very difficult to be chief." Finally he said, "I shall not be chief." It was not easy for him to simply sit in one spot for 10 days. "I see", he said, "chiefs have a hard time." He continued to think so. He wished the people to be all killed.

There was another person, Wī'sa'kä'ᴀ, who was a demigod (ma ne to wa ᴀ le ta we si ᴀ). He continued to instruct the people, it is said, because these their foes from without were going about giving each other tobacco (as a pledge) to join in exterminating this one nation. "Let us kill all these Meskwakies. Let us cut off their retreat", was said. And these peoples began to gather to camp. They camped all about (the Meskwaki). "Surely it is a large village", these peoples said among themselves. "Why they will surely kill us all" (the Meskwakies) said among themselves. "Why if we were brave warriors if these men tried anything we could strike them down, we surely could strike them down, I think." This one man kept on saying, "Yes", but the others made no response. Just as it was dawn the men were fired on, and they began to hold a council. This Wi te ko ka ᴀ ᴀ said, "I am going to fight. I must fight right here. That is what I think", so he said. "I shall be the first", said this WâpA'saiyᴀ (White Robe). "Well!" thought Wi te ko ka ᴀ ᴀ, "we probably shall be destroyed", so he thought. "Let the young men at once build a fence", the old men said among themselves. At that time the people, that is, the old men, fought furiously, and the old men shot each other down, and were destroyed. And these young men also went off and built a fence. And exactly when they had completed the fence those old men were all slain. And they, the youths, rushed to attack each other. It was not only these, but also nearly all those very old men who could not get around. And those old men were all killed. Then the young men fought against each other. Soon, after 10 days, they were made to feel hunger. And they held a council. This was somewhere northeast of the body of water called "Green Lake" (i. e., Green Bay). They were made to suffer cruelly and they were hungry. They desired greatly to know what to do. Now these members of the Bear gens were there. And one of them spoke to the War Chiefs. "I shall put them asleep", he said, "I shall make it stormy", they were told. And this man, it is said, went to employ ceremonial attendants to dip this wolf hide a little so that they could get through thereby, and so that it

would not be known whither they went. And he said, "You ceremonial attendants are to dip it only a little (in the lake)." That
verily is what they did. They dipped it too much and they became
very much frightened. That is what happened to them, according
to tradition. As soon as the wolf had been dipped, lo! these nations
were fast asleep; they had been made to sleep, it is said, by this
Ke ke gi mo A who was worshiping at the time. Then they started
to walk. Sight was impossible as soon as they had come out. And
this Ke ke gi mo A was the first when they were moving, but this
member of the War Chiefs (Ke le yo ma wa) was the first when they
went outside their encampment where they had planned to meet
each other. That, it is said, was the only way in which they were
able to get together. You may know there was a rock shelter
toward which they were fleeing and which they entered. "They
will overtake us", this party said among themselves, "but we shall
kill many of them." And the next day he (Ke le yo ma wa ?
Ke ke gi mo A ?) was overtaken. That is what happened to them.
(And their foes were defeated.) In the north at that time their
grain was mature. That is what those who fled into the rock shelter
say. At that time they were approached, seen, and attacked by
these alien men.

This lake, it is said, was very dangerous. Whenever anyone fell
in he sank to the bottom. It was dangerous and feared. And
when their foes came to attack them they all sank to the bottom.
That is what they say among themselves.

Finally when they went back, they all halted in their speed in
the journey to where they were fleeing. There is no further information regarding them in respect to their flight.

Now these men were very angry, and they were let alone and
they departed.

Now, it is said, soon again they were surrounded by the Sioux,
Chippewa, and Menominee. That is what happened to them. It
was at A se na na ko ki where they were surrounded. Yet not even
one of them was slain. That is what is said of them. They surely
killed all their foes.

Now these friends were great fighters. Yet soon they gave up.
They became tired of fighting. This WâpA'saiyA (White Robe) broke
his bow and was captured. And he was interrogated by his friend.
"You may go, my friend," he said to him. So the man (WApA'saiyA)
was captured. One old man recognized the other, for he looked as
his son had looked; and WâpA'saiyA's friend married the old man's
son's wife. And as for this WâpA'saiyA (White Robe) he was led
away. For food he was fed his own flesh which was slashed off.
Finally he was all slashed. And, it is said, one old man, a very old
man, came and threw hot ashes in this warrior's face. And twigs
were set on fire at his feet and the post to which he was bound.

This old man was told, "I shall burn with this village." And this same old man was terribly whipped. "What are you beginning to say to him, for he is a manitou? You are injuring us." And these disappeared.

Thereupon this one who was married soon went hunting (as was supposed); he did not halt; he went home. When he arrived he told what had happened to the other. "I would not have fought, if he had stood about," this man said. "I shall go and fetch them," he said. And he went thither. No one was able to accompany him. He went alone. He took his wife and children there. After they camped they made a pit in the center of the wigwam. And, it is said, the next day, when these people (the foe) woke up, it seems that there was a Meskwaki camp where they dwelt. "They have brought their bodies for soup," he said. And these men rushed upon them. They fell in the pit in the dwelling and he slaughtered them. Finally these men gave up after nearly all had been slain. That is what these Meskwakies did. And they moved hurriedly and fasted earnestly. Even the little children were made to fast and were not fed for 10 days. They merely opened their mouths and were hungry for 10 days.

And this man who was called "Ke le yo ma wa" was ever going on the warpath. But always brought only a very few captives. And this man called Wi te ko ka ᴀ ᴀ killed all whenever he came upon a village. So the Meskwakies did their best. And he did not fear even many Sioux. That is why these other Indians live so far away from the Meskwakies, because these drove the other Indians away. The Chippewa, Menominee, and Sioux fled to the north. That is what they did. Today they are very much afraid. And they do not come here to visit. So it is.

Well, I shall repeat today a little of what they did. The people all made mistakes in the past. And they made a mistake when they came and attacked the Meskwakies. Surely they did what I have narrated.

Well, this Ke le yo ma wa began to go on the warpath. These Meskwakies stood about a stump of a tree and when he came they clubbed all his captives to death. That is what they did. And he had the most songs. There are many songs connected with this sacred pack. They use them still. The songs belonging to that sacred pack got them through their difficulties. That is how it is. What I tell today is not a lie. There is much of this story.

Another thing they do is this:[9] This ceremonial attendant is selected. He is selected 8 days in advance. "Well, ceremonial attendant, I appoint you to go about and inform those whom you serve as a ceremonial attendant", this person who is a member of the Wolf gens is told. For 8 days he looks for chickens. Whatever they get

---

[9] See fig. 9 for a diagram of the festival in summer. I think no. 8 should be placed beneath no. 7.

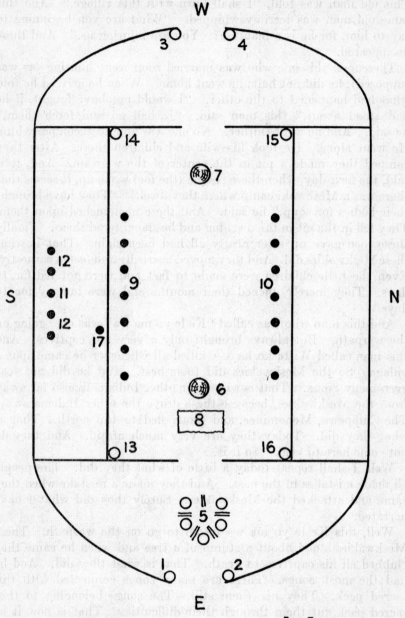

1-2-3-4· DOOR POSTS
5 - FIRE PLACE
6-7 - MAIN PILLARS
8 - SACRED PACK CON-   17- SPEAKER
   TAINING WOLF HIDE

9 - KĪ⁽CKŌ DANCERS
10 - TŌ⁽KĀN DANCERS
11 - DRUMMER
12 - SINGERS
13-14-15-16 - PILLARS

FIGURE 9.—Summer performance of "When the War Chiefs Worship the Wolf"
(same informant as for figure 4).

they bring them there to pluck them. That indeed is what they say to each other, and it is what they do. At the time they gather and bring their offerings. So at this point this should be a topic for me to talk about. And they bring their pets—chickens. And some squirrels, and some ground hogs, some pumpkins, some dried corn, some corn dumplings, a single hog. Usually the leading one offers the hog. Thereupon these ceremonial attendants pluck the chickens. Some singe the squirrels, and some kill the hog. That is what they do in regular order. That is what I wish to tell, though there is still much to be told. And the next morning these ceremonial attendants begin to boil the squirrels and the hog. They especially dedicate this single hog, the corn dumplings, and hog's head to the wolf. Formerly, it is said, it was a bear's head. Thus they did.

And when this fresh meat is boiled these men who are celebrants of the feast are addressed at length. The leading ceremonial attendant is told by this fellow, "Now you (pl.) are to prepare a drum, using this hide." The leading ceremonial attendant is a member of the Wolf gens. "Very well", he replies. Thereupon, it is said, he goes and directs others to help him. These will be a member of the Feathered (Thunder) gens, a member of the Bear gens, and a member of the Dirty Little Ani. If these men are absent he might employ anyone. There is much of this ceremony. As soon as their drum is tied up, then the one who casts tobacco begins to tie it in a buckskin (placing it near the wolf hide). And this wolf hide is taken down and hung there; as soon as this one who is to cast tobacco in the fire has spoken tobacco is tied in buckskin.

And they do not celebrate this gens festival every day. They celebrate it twice a year—in spring and in the harvest time. That is what they do, always.

This story and the songs have been handed down by tradition throughout the years from a long time ago, before the white man came here. But today for the first time they are written down on paper.

Surely it is a most interesting story. Even I should look at it with interest after it is printed in a book. Of course as I tell this I merely narrate it. It is not my story, but what I heard about this long ago when I was a boy.

Well, now this leader begins to speak to this Spirit of Fire. And this is what he says, "Well, my grandfather, Spirit of Fire, I give you this tobacco to smoke, and you Whose Eyes Bulge In The Smoke-Hole", he said to those manitous, "your fellow manitous have already spoken to you and ordered you to watch and see what manitous we remember whenever we worship. Today verily we who belong to the War Chiefs gens in our worship remember the wolf hide. That verily is why we give you this tobacco to smoke. In whatever ways the wolf hide thought of the one called 'Ke le yo ma wa' [=KepäyōmāwA] you will now bless him. Those indeed are as many ways as we desire for him.

That verily is why we now ask that the land of this our chief shall rest securely and that no evil enter it, and that it always be well. You will bless us that way because of our tobacco. And also whoever from without goes about speaking evil against our chief's town, may he end his thought prematurely. Oh, if he thinks contrariwise too much, he shall instead curse himself." That is how this man spoke. "This is as far as I shall address you today, my grandfather, Spirit of Fire. In return you will bless us. You will replace our kettle with one slice whenever the manitou places war on his land."

That, it seems, is what this man said to the Spirit of Fire. He usually was the first speaker. That is what I tell today.

Then he arises and eventually goes and sits comfortably where those who are celebrating the feast sit. He starts to speak. "Well, you must eventually speak (i. e., pray), my grandchildren. You must begin to sing. It will be evening." This is what he says to them. "Now indeed you are to begin to sing quickly. You must sing in a circle."

They say there were 122 songs, but not now.

Well! of a surety the ceremonial attendants are told, "Come, hand me the flute, ceremonial attendants." They begin to sing after they have beaten the drum. They begin to sing after this fellow has beaten the drum. First they point this flute to east, south, west, and north, blowing it. "Come, now hand us our drum" is said. Then the ceremonial attendants hand it to the one who is to beat the drum. When he has sat down with it those who are to sing sit down with gourds (rattles). Thereupon this drummer strikes the drum four times in advance. And when they have sung the aforementioned man tells how Ke le yo ma wa was first blessed. "You will hold a ghost feast for me", he must have said. Verily these Meskwakies will never forget him whenever they worship. Before any one of these ceremonial attendants comes they always eat a little something. They hold a ghost feast for the one blessed. And they are fed when they are in the house of worship before they sing. Then indeed their plans are first completed. That is what I say about them. They surely have a hard time and suffer. That is the way with these peoples. No one knows how to sing all these songs. Those who are in the habit of singing remained seated when they have sung.

Thereupon one game animal is halved and these men and the ceremonial attendants are those who eat first. They are donated this game animal. This might be a skunk, it might be a raccoon, it might be a duck. It should be one of these. And they eat in pairs. That is how they stand. One is standing; he eats first. One merely remains standing. Back in the rear is where one eats. They eat alternately (?). The one who eats first then goes and stands in the rear.

There are two sets of songs which are used (eating and dancing ones). But I cannot write the songs. I am too much afraid, I suppose. I might write them some other time, but not now.

Now before the people were surrounded there were many. That is what they formerly were in the habit of saying.

At one time the Great Manitou's son saw with pleasure the youths playing la crosse and other pastimes. And he asked that he might go and live with them. "Now you might do something wrong. For they do excessive evil", the Great Manitou said to his son. "No. For I shall abide in the chief's dwelling", the latter said. So it was that the Great Manitou was done wrong. "Well, you shall do that very thing", he said to his son. And the Great Manitou's son was born as a boy in the chief's dwelling. He was treated very meanly by the one who raised him and was whipped severely all the time. And the Great Manitou discovered that his son was weeping and took him back, it is said, for he was unwilling for his son not to be well treated. So the boy died and was taken back by his father. And the boy's skin was made red. "In this way probably your parents will not abuse you. And he sent him back again. He was sent back in the dwelling of a member of the War Chiefs gens. So he was born there. "Now fast, WâpA'saiyA", he was told. "Why should I fast? For I dream many dreams as I sleep", he said to his parents, and they ceased saying anything to him. He was very mean, they say. Soon he accompanied a war party. He and his friend went together. His friend's name was Na sa li lya ta. At that time they were just young men and doughty. They even had war clubs with them when they departed. They always made the Sioux wail when they slew them. They saughtered and killed many. It was what the people desired. These did what the people desired them to do. One was naturally brave, the other was brave from fasting. They knew each other well. They were friends because they were so much alike. That is what the people did, so the members of the War Chiefs gens are in the habit of telling. The son of the Great Manitou came to live with them in person. That is what they tell in between times at the feast to make it interesting.

"Well, it is getting late", they say to each other. "Well, begin to sing quickly. Hand us our flute. You will hand us the drum at the same time", is what they say. Thereupon they begin to sing. As soon as they have sung the second time then the Mystic Men worship the ceremonial dolls (me si ne ni a i; obviate pl.), and they eat. Also members of the Rabbit Society (me dwe wa dge A ki). They are very particular. Those inside may not go out, nor those seated outside may not enter during eating or prayer. There are watchers on each end of the doors who watch those who eat (to see that these rules are not broken). I do not know what they say: It is merely about the sacred hide which belongs to the pack (le ne si wi ya).

"Eat ye", they are accustomed to say. They dip their fingers in before they start to eat. The one seated at the east does so first; (and it continues in a ring). Then they eat. After they have eaten they eventually sit down comfortably where they are sitting. They were seated in the center of the dwelling during the eating. Then they begin to dance. They are dancing for the third time. And after they have danced three times they give the hog's head to their nieces (sisters' daughters); these are usually head dancers; they give the hog to their sisters-in-law. And the food is served then to any-one. They eat heartily. They have an enjoyable time. When they have danced the very last time a very brave warrior speaks (i. e., prays). He prays for those celebrating the festival. That is what they do, it is said. "Oh, all to whom I am related, those who are worshiping", the speaker says, "also those who serve as ceremonial attendants, all ye to whom I am related", he says, "those who light the tobacco which has been brought, also all to whom I am related", he says, "also, so be it, the venerable one of these celebrants who was blessed by the manitou and their grandfathers who has passed this down to us. This is what our grandfathers said to us and what they desired. Surely they have done well in remembering the one reputed to be their grandfather (i. e., the wolf); surely they have done well today", says the one by whom they are addressed. And that is as far as he speaks. It is as far as I have heard.

APPENDIX: WI TE KO KA A A

Now a man lived with his father and he (the man) had two boys and a wife. Every time the people went on the warpath he went along; but he was only a man, and was never spoken of as in any way distinguished. Many times the other men were spoken of as being renowned, but that did not happen to him. Well, once when they were going to war, he was told by his father, "Why do you not cease accompanying them, for you are credited with nothing when deeds of war are spoken of at gatherings? Verily I shall go along. You will see to what an extent I shall be hailed as a man", he was told by his father. "You indeed will be slain", he was told. Later on indeed when there was talk of war his father went along, and when the warriors returned his father also returned. His father had gone to war successfully. "That is how you should have been talked of", he was told. His father was arrayed so gorgeously that his son sat with bowed head. His father was completely clad in the finery of a warrior, for he was indeed a great warrior. "My son, you might become a warrior. 'Fast', I have told you", he was told. "Even some women have become warrior women", he was told. "When-ever you go to war I shall accompany you", he was told.

So he began to fast earnestly and camped by himself. For several years he lived alone far off from the village. Then he began to save feathers. He tied them in grass bags, and finally had many of them. "What is he going to do with them?" was asked. Eventually his wickiup was full of them, and there were even some around the exterior.

When the people moved the women who had children carried them on their backs and those who had no children packed other things on their backs. Finally they reached where they were to camp. Soon some of the men who looked about discovered there was a Sioux village not far away; it was over the hills in a valley. There were many tipis. It was smoky. The Meskwakies were outnumbered and surrounded. So this man took his feathers which he had fastened on long poles in a row; they were a kind of flag. He implanted these poles in the ground around a very large and long wickiup. And the Sioux also had their feather flags. As soon as the Sioux saw this wickiup decorated with the feather flags they gave war whoops and surrounded it. All the Meskwakies ran into this wickiup. The man had told his tribesmen what he was going to do: He first was going to get two scalps at first, but when he got four he could save the people. He covered the wickiup. These feathers had given the man some kind of power; so it was that he got the better of the Sioux, their enemy, and he at once got four scalps; and he so frightened the Sioux that they ran in every direction. Thereupon he struck the wickiup four times as hard as he could; and the foe ran all the faster.

After the fight was over they looked for food to eat. And after the old man was filled he went out to see the dead. They were lying all over on the ground, and even in their own dwellings. "Well, well", he said and smiled because his son at last had become a hero, a true warrior who had saved the people from the enemy.

And two young men said they were going about and see the dead in the Sioux village. So they started. Now this brave man had told them not to bother the dead bodies, not to kick them, nor say anything to them. And so the two young men walked around the village. In the very center was a beautiful tipi. "This must be the chief's tipi", they said. When they looked inside they beheld the brave man's father pretending to be married to the chief's daughter, who was a young girl. The old man had taken off his moccasins, and was standing about barefooted and was talking to the dead as if she were his wife. And these two young men saw him when they peeped in, but he did not hear or see them watching him. They left the door flap open and ran back and told this old man's son what his father was doing. So he sent these young men back to frighten him. They hid and pretended that the body had come back to life. The old man jumped up and ran off as fast as he could from the ghost village. He ran into his son's lodge out of breath. His son ordered a strong whip to be fetched. So it was. Thereupon he whipped his father severely. The old man cried out that it hurt. "I want it to hurt. I have a good reason for doing this. You are not a child. Look at your gray hair." And they pushed his head. Whereat he was ashamed.

After the war the village people were getting ready to move back where their village had been. And this old man was standing around barefooted. "May I go back for my moccasins?" he asked his son. "Are they where your father-in-law is? Hurry and fetch them", he was told.

And the people moved away. When they arrived at their old village they feasted bounteously. The meat was very fine. Had it not been for this brave the Sioux would have killed them all. The people had brought back many scalps. And this young man was thought the greatest warrior of his people.

Now one day the old man acted as if he were ill. "What do you wish", said his son. "I wish to fill a pipe and smoke it." "Well, can't you?" said his son.

And this brave man called all the women to cook for a great feast. He called all the women of the village to come and eat. After they had eaten he asked them to make roofing out of flat flag weeds; they were to use these by making them into mattings to cover a wickiup. He had a pile of dried flag weeds, and they were woven into mats in a single day.

After this the old man was good for nothing; he simply lay about smoking all the while.

And the following day this brave man had his wickiup moved; it was entirely new, and it was a very long wickiup. His father was now an old man and all he could do was to smoke.

While this man was living happily some Sioux who were on the warpath saw his wickiup and planned to attack the village early the following morning. But this man knew it, for he had seen them and had heard what they were saying. So he was prepared. He did as he had done previously. He put out his feather flags and covered his wickiup with the feathers. And the following morning before daybreak, very early in the morning the Sioux prepared to make an attack. This man's name was Wi te ko ka A. He had told the men who were going to help him to pound on the wickiup as hard as they could. So while this warrior went out the others stayed and pounded on the wickiup. It made a big noise, as if guns were being fired. So every time the Sioux came close they became frightened and they ran off; so they could not attack the long wickiup. And this Wi te ko ka A went about killing a band of Sioux consisting of warriors only. So he again was the brave man. Every time the Sioux threw a sharp ax at him or a war club it did not hit him: He would catch it and throw it back again. Finally he cornered the leading men, killed them all, and scalped them. So the Meskwakies were left alone.

LIST OF WORKS CITED

BLOOMFIELD, LEONARD. Menomini Texts. Publ. Amer. Ethn. Soc., vol. XII'
New York, 1928.

BOAS, FRANZ. Tsimshian Mythology. Thirty-first Ann. Rept. Bur. Amer.
Ethn., Washington, 1916.

FORSYTH, THOMAS. An Account of the Manners and Customs of the Sauk and
Fox Nations of Indian Tradition. *In* Blair, E. H., The Indian Tribes
of the Upper Mississippi Valley and Region of the Great Lakes, vol. II,
Cleveland, 1912.

FORTUNE, REO F. Omaha Secret Societies. Col. Univ. Cont. to Anthrop.,
vol. XIV, New York, 1932.

JONES, WILLIAM. Ojibwa Tales from the North Shore of Lake Superior. Journ.
Amer. Folk-Lore, vol. 29, pp. 368–391. Lancaster and New York, 1916.

—————— The Algonkin Manitou. Jour. Amer. Folk-Lore, vol. 18, pp. 183–190.
New York and Boston, 1905.

—————— Algonquian (Fox). Revised by Truman Michelson. Handbook of
American Indian Languages, Bur. Amer. Ethn., Bull. 40, pt. 1, pp.
735–873, Washington, 1911.

—————— Fox Texts. Publ. Amer. Ethn. Soc., vol. I, Leyden, 1907.

MICHELSON, TRUMAN. The Mythical Origin of the White Buffalo Dance of the
Fox Indians. Fortieth Ann. Rept. Bur. Amer. Ethn., pp. 23–289,
Washington, 1925.

—————— The Autobiography of a Fox Indian Woman. Ibid., pp. 291–349.

—————— Notes on Fox Mortuary Customs and Beliefs. Ibid., pp. 351–496.

—————— List of Stems. Ibid., pp. 616–658.

—————— The Owl Sacred Pack of the Fox Indians. Bull. 72, Bur. Amer. Ethn.,
Washington, 1921.

—————— Notes on the Buffalo-Head Dance of the Thunder Gens of the Fox Indians.
Bull 87, Bur. Amer. Ethn., Washington, 1928.

—————— A Sketch of the Buffalo Dance of the Bear Gens of the Fox Indians.
Bull. 95, Bur. Amer. Ethn., pp. 1–41, Washington, 1930.

—————— Note on Fox Gens Festivals. Proc. Twenty-third Int. Cong. Americanists, 1928, pp. 545–546, New York, 1930.

—————— Notes on the Great Sacred Pack of the Thunder Gens of the Fox Indians.
Ibid., pp. 43–176.

—————— Notes on the Fox WÂPANŌWIWENI. Bull. 105, Bur. Amer. Ethn., Washington, 1932.

SKINNER, ALANSON. Observations on the Ethnology of the Sauk Indians. Bull.
Pub. Mus. Milwaukee, vol. 5, no. 1, Milwaukee, 1923.

UNITED STATES STATUTES AT LARGE, vol. VII, Treaties, Boston, 1848.

WARD, DUREN J. H. The Meskwaki People of Today. Iowa Journ. Hist., vol.
IV, pp. 190–219, Iowa City, 1906.

INDEX

	Page
ADDRESS TO SPIRITS	85–86
ALGONQUIANS, CENTRAL, mention of dance of	13
"ALL LITTLE MEDICINE BUNDLES," organization called	12
A'PENÄWÄNÄ'A, sacred pack of the Thunder gens	13
BEAR GENS:	
ceremonial color of	29
mention of	8, 10, 12, 13, 14, 15, 16, 17, 39, 50, 82
reciprocal burials of	65
taboos of	64
BEAVER GENS:	
reciprocal burials of	65
taboo of	64
BERRIES, ceremony connected with	66
BIRD DANCE, mention of	13, 15, 17
BLACK BEAR, a division of the Bear gens	29
BLOOMFIELD, cited	2
BOAS, FRANZ, reference to work of	2
BROWN, TOM, translation by	1
BUFFALO DANCE OF THE BEAR GENS, reference to	12
BUFFALO HEAD DANCE, mention of	13, 15, 16
BUFFALO, MYTHICAL:	
of the east	44, 53
of the west	40, 44
BUFFALO SOCIETY MEDICINE BUNDLES, organization called	12, 13, 14, 15
BUFFALOES:	
mythical, under the earth	49
taboo concerning	24, 25
BURIAL CUSTOMS. See MORTUARY CUSTOMS.	
CALENDAR OF THE SAUK AND FOX	3
CARDINAL POINTS, orientation of	44
CATAMENIAL SOCIETY, reference to	12, 14, 15, 16, 17

	Page
CEREMONIAL ATTENDANTS, duties of	50, 58, 59, 62, 82, 87
CEREMONY, pattern of	9
CHIEFTAINSHIP, succession in	29
CHILDBIRTH, treatment in	62–63
CHIPMUNK, tales concerning	2–3, 75
CLEANLINESS, observance of	62
CLOTHING, rule concerning	67
CORN, ceremonial feast of	66
CUSTOMS OF THE FOX INDIANS	62–67
DEMI-GOD, etymology of Fox word for	11
DEMOCRACY, FOX, theoretical, not actual	8
DIRTY LITTLE ANI:	
mention of	12
organization called	14, 15, 64
reciprocal burials of	65
taboos of	64
DREAM DANCE, mention of	13
DREAMS, religious	24
DRUM DANCE, mention of	13
EAGLE GENS:	
mention of	12, 13, 15, 39
reciprocal burials of	65
taboo of	64
FASTING:	
custom of	65
dreams caused by	24
religious	79
FEATHERED GENS, reference to	38, 39, 42
FINGERNAILS, custom concerning	62
FISH GENS:	
mention of	12, 13, 14, 15
other name for	2
reciprocal burials of	65
taboos of	64
FISHER, MARGARET W., theoretical exogamy proved by	2
FLAG CEREMONY, resemblance of, to other ceremonial	9–10
FORSYTH, THOMAS:	
cited	3, 4, 6
list of months given by	4–5

Page

FORTUNE, R. F., cited_____ 8
FOUR, the ceremonial number__ 18,
    25, 26, 27, 29, 31, 32, 33, 36, 45,
    58, 60, 63, 67, 79, 80, 81.
Fox Indians:
    culture hero of_____ 11
    dance introduced among___ 13
    reference to tales of_____ 2–3
GENS, EXTINCT, taboos of_____ 64
GENTES:
    differences among_____ 65
    reciprocal burials of_____ 65
GREAT MANITOU, mention of___ 34,
    35, 47, 48
GREAT SACRED PACK OF THE
    THUNDER GENS, reference to_ 12,
    13, 15, 17
GREEN, a ceremonial color_____ 21, 29
GREEN BUFFALO:
    a mythical being_____ 31,
    32, 34, 41, 45, 50, 56
    legend of_____ 18–62
GREEN BUFFALO DANCE OF THE
    WOLF GENS, mention of_____ 1
HAIRDRESSING, rule concerning_ 67
"HE WHO KNOWS INNER
    THOUGHTS":
    a mythical being_____ 55
    See also "HE WHOSE EYES
        BULGE IN THE SMOKE-
        HOLE."
"HE WHOSE EYES BULGE IN THE
    SMOKE-HOLE," the manitou__ 40,
    52, 85, 86
HEROES, LEGENDARY, use of the
    term_____ 11
INFORMANTS, anonymous_____ 8
INTERLOCKING "DIRECTORATES":
    discussion of_____ 8, 9, 12
    examples of_____ 12
JONES, HENRY:
    acknowledgment to_____ 3
    appreciation of_____ 4
JONES, WILLIAM:
    acknowledgment to_____ 3
    appreciation of_____ 4
    cited_____ 2, 6, 65
    list of months given by____ 5
    mention of_____ 2
KEPĀYŌMĀWA, short form of
    name_____ 11
KICKAPOO, culture hero of_____ 11

Page

KICKAPOO, MEXICAN:
    month names of_____ 6
    reference to_____ 2
KINDLY CHIEFS GENS:
    mention of_____ 14
    taboo of_____ 64
KIYANA, ALFRED, informant___ 8,
    9, 10, 11, 13, 14, 15
LABOR, division of_____ 67
LEGEND OF WI TE KO KA A A__ 116–118
LINCOLN, HARRY:
    acknowledgment to_____ 8, 9
    corrections made by_____ 6
    text obtained from_____ 1
LINGUISTIC NOTES_____ 13, 76–78
MANITOU OF THE EAST, reference
    to_____ 59
MARRIAGE CUSTOMS_____ 2, 63
MEDICAL PRACTICES_____ 67
MENOMINEE, reference to tale
    of_____ 2–3
MENSTRUAL CUSTOMS_____ 48, 62
MENSTRUATING SOCIETY:
    information gathered on___ 2
    origin myth of_____ 63–64
    reciprocal burials of_____ 65
MESKWAKIES:
    mention of_____ 17, 28
    synonym of Foxes_____ 17
MONTHS:
    comparison of lists of_____ 4–6
    discussion of names of_____ 3–7
    lists of names of_____ 3, 7, 73
MORNING BIRDS, taboos of____ 64
MORTUARY CUSTOMS____ 65, 65–66, 67
MOURNING CUSTOMS_____ 65, 67
MYTH OF THE MONTHS, transla-
    tion of_____ 7
NAMING CUSTOMS_____ 10
NORTHERN BUFFALO, a mythi-
    cal being_____ 40
OJIBWA, reference to tale of____ 2–3
ORIGIN MYTHS:
    formulas of_____ 9
    pattern of_____ 9
PA'CITŌNĪGWA:
    chief of Meskwakies_____ 17
    information furnished by__ 65
PEYOTE CULT, mention of_____ 15, 16
PORTRAITS, objection to_____ 67
POTAWATOMI:
    dance introduced by_____ 13
    mention of dance of_____ 15

POTAWATOMI, PRAIRIE, culture | Page
hero of ---------------------- | 11
POWESHIEK, HORACE, paraphrase by ------------------- | 1
POWESHIEK, IDA, assistance of -- | 8, 9
RED STONE PIPE CEREMONY, mention of -------------- 12, 13, 15
RELIGION DANCE, reference to- | 13, 15, 17

ROCK-MAN, a mythical being -- | 31
SACRED PACK:
of the Bear gens, reference to ---------------------- | 12, 15
of the Thunder gens, reference to ----------------- | 12
Sāgimā'kwäwä, sacred pack of Bear gens ------------------- | 15
SAUK, culture hero of ---------- | 11
SAUK AND FOX, list of moons of- | 3
SEDUCTION, punishment for ---- | 63
SIOUX, reference to ----------- | 28, 60
SMOKING CEREMONIAL --------- | 63
SNOW BALL, IDA, name of Ida Poweshiek ----------------- | 8
SONGS, words of -------------- 41–44, 46, 50, 56, 66, 94, 95
SPEECH, TERMINAL, of "When the War Chiefs Worship the Wolf" ---------------------- | 86–87
SPIRIT OF FIRE:
offering to --------------- | 47
reference to -------------- | 40, 41, 45, 54, 55, 79, 85
SPOTTED FACE SOCIETY, mention of --------------------- | 15
SUNNY BUFFALO, a mythical being ---------------- 39, 44, 53, 54
TEETH, custom concerning ----- | 62
TEN, a ceremonial number ----- | 79
"THE ONE WHOM THE MOONS BLESSED".
an origin myth ----------- | 68–75
when collected ----------- | 1
"THOSE NAMED AFTER THE BUFFALO":
reciprocal burials of ------- | 65
taboos of ----------------- | 64
"THOSE WHO WORSHIP THE LITTLE SPOTTED BUFFALO", mention of ---------------------- | 12

THUNDER DANCE OF THE BEAR | Page
GENS, mention of -------- | 13, 14, 17
THUNDER GENS:
Great Sacred Pack of ----- | 17
mention of --- 12, 13, 14, 15, 16, 17
reciprocal burials of ------- | 65
taboos of ----------------- | 64
TOBACCO, as an offering ------- | 19, 20, 22, 25, 26, 45, 47
WAR CHIEFS GENS:
list of months by informant of ---------------------- | 6
mention of --------------- | 7, 8, 9, 10, 12, 13, 14, 16, 17, 21, 22, 23, 37, 39, 50, 58, 59, 79.
reciprocal burials of ------- | 65
"WARRIOR WOMEN", customs of- | 66
WARRIORS, custom concerning-- | 66
WELLS, ATTORNEY, acknowledgment to --------------------- | 3
"WHEN THE WAR CHIEFS RAISE THE FLAG":
full name of Flag ceremony- | 9
mention of ------ 12, 14, 15, 16, 17
"WHEN THE WAR CHIEFS WORSHIP THE BUFFALOES", mention of ----------- 12, 13, 14, 15, 17
"WHEN THE WAR CHIEFS WORSHIP THE WOLF":
a ceremonial organization-- | 9
collection of material on--- | 7
data on------------------- | 9
legend of ----------------- | 79–82
mention of --------- 12, 13, 14, 15
miscellaneous information on----------- 97–102, 102–116
summer performance----- | 82–84, 87–88, 88–91, 91–93
winter performance------- | 84–85
"WHEN THE WAR CHIEFS WORSHIP THE WOLF AND GIVE A DANCE", members of -------- | 11–17
"WHEN THE WOLF GENS WORSHIPS THE WHITE WOLF", mention of ----------------- | 13
WHISTLING, taboo concerning-- | 67
"WHITE BUFFALO DANCE OF THE WAR CHIEFS", other name of- | 12
WHITE BUFFALO SOCIETY, regulations of ----------------- | 64–65
WHITE ROBE, treaty signed by-- | 11

WHITE WOLVES: Page
    burial custom of_____ 65
    customs of_____ 66
    information gathered on___ 2
    taboo of_____ 64
WIDOWERS, customs concern-
    ing_____ 65
WIDOWS, customs concerning__ 65
WINTRY BUFFALO, a mythical
    being_____ 44, 54

                      Page
WĪʻSʻAKAʻA, mention of_____ 73, 75
WI TE KO KA A A, legend concern-
    ing_____ 116–118
WOLF DANCE OF WAR CHIEFS
    GENS_____ 93–97
WOLF GENS:
    mention of_____ 40, 58, 62, 82
    origin myth of ceremony of_ 18–62
    reciprocal burials of_____ 65
    taboos of_____ 64

○